"Joel Fitzpatrick wants to help boys grow up to be passionate spiritual men. But he knows that simply learning a list of godly character traits is not the key to manliness. *Between Us Guys* makes clear that what sons need most is to know and love the God who became a man to save them. I'm really excited to recommend this devotional for dads of boys in our church."

> **Jared Kennedy**, Pastor of Operations and Families at Sojourn Church Midtown, Louisville, KY; author of *The Beginner's Gospel Story Bible*

"William Butler Yeats, in his 1929 poem *Coole Park*, used these words to describe a particular man: 'There one that ruffled in a manly pose, For all his timid heart.' Everywhere we turn today, the fallout of 'ruffling men' is hard to ignore. Men are 'ruffling' and 'posing' because, deep down, they have no clue who they are. Within the heart of every man is the question, 'Do I have what it takes?' and, for most men, this question has never come close to being answered. Ideally, fathers help sons answer this question, but the fathers of most men are still looking for the answer themselves. *Between Us Guys: Life-Changing Conversations for Dads and Sons* is a book that is transformative for fathers *and* sons because it helps both answer the 'Do I have what it takes?' question. This book calls dads and sons into the true fellowship of manhood where ruffling and posing are no longer necessary."

> **Tray Lovvorn**, Podcast host, speaker, and cofounder of Undone Redone, Inc.

"Life is hectic. Distractions abound. Meaningful conversations don't just happen. Thankfully, Joel Fitzpatrick not only encourages fathers and father figures to cut through the clutter of daily life and engage their sons in real conversations, but he also equips them to do it. These fast-paced, engaging devotionals help dads point their sons to Jesus. As a pastor and father of three sons, I could not be more grateful."

> **Kevin Labby**, Senior Pastor, Willow Creek Presbyterian Church, Winter Springs, FL

"'So be strong, act like a man' (1 Kings 2:2). In our age the words of King David while on his deathbed to his son Solomon would be considered offensive. In this work, Joel realizes that sad reality and treats the subject of 'what is a man' with the utmost of care while never backing down on what a man really is. His little work teaches men to talk to their sons, telling them that a man is a broken person who looks to Christ as their only hope for salvation while trying to live their vocations by serving their neighbors in love, freely. If you are a father with sons, don't miss out on this invaluable resource."

Scott L. Keith, Executive Director, 1517 The Legacy Project; author of *Being Dad: Father as a Picture of God's Grace*

"Some of the most life-shaping moments of my life were spent one on one with my father. This wonderful book brought me right back to those conversations. It's not just a book about 'the sex talk' that fathers dread. It's a book about talking to your son as a fellow guy. It's about having conversations that will never leave him. It's about pointing boys to Christ in everything. I highly recommend it."

Daniel Emery Price, Director of Christ Hold Fast; author of *Scandalous Stories: A Sort of Commentary on Parables*

"Here's a book for each of us dads who has found it hard to start those most important conversations we want to have with our boys. Joel not only knows how to get us talking, he reminds us what is most important—and that's Jesus."

Jack Klumpenhower, Author of *Show Them Jesus*

"When it comes to dads building a close relationship with their sons, sometimes the hardest part is knowing where to start. *Between Us Guys* is a valuable means for connecting fathers and sons. It provides both the substance and easy avenues for fathers and sons to have meaningful conversations. I believe that any father who reads through *Between Us Guys* with his sons will grow closer to them and their God."

Cameron Cole, Director of Children, Youth, and Family, The Cathedral Church of the Advent; founding chairman of Rooted Ministry; coeditor of *Gospel-Centered Youth Ministry: A Practical Guide*; and author of *Therefore I Have Hope: 12 Truths That Comfort, Sustain, and Redeem in Tragedy*

"Attention Dads! In your hand is a tool that will guide you into a deeper relationship with your son and draw both of you into a deeper relationship with Jesus. *Between Us Guys* is filled with stimulating thoughts from Scripture on many rhythms of life (work, play, money, sex, . . . even failure!), which then tee up dads for great talks with their sons. If you're looking for something fresh, practical and gospel-saturated, something that includes solid discussion questions and helpful activities—buy this book and start making memories with your boy!"

Dave Harvey, President, Sojourn Network; teaching pastor at Summit Church, Naples; founder of AmICalled.com; author

"Since I'm neither a dad nor a son (obviously!), you might be wondering why I'd endorse a book like this. It's because I know the author very well. In fact, I've known him well since the day he was born. I've watched him grow up, marry, have children, and become a pastor. And I've watched him parent his son and his daughter, and I love the way he loves them. He's qualified to write this book for you because he lives this kind of life with his son every day. Moms, pick this up as a gift for your husbands. Dads, pick this up as a starting place for meaningful conversations with your sons. I know this author. He's the real deal."

Elyse Fitzpatrick, Author of *Give Them Grace*

"Honest. Insightful. Christ-centered. Those words sum up well this splendid gem of a book by Joel Fitzpatrick. Drawing on his own experience as a dad, he leads us into wise and critical conversations to have with our sons. My own son is now eighteen. I wish I'd had this book early in his life as a guide on our own journey together."

Chad Bird, Author and speaker

BETWEEN
US
GUYS

BETWEEN US GUYS

Life-Changing Conversations for Dads and Sons

Joel Fitzpatrick

New
Growth
Press
WWW.NEWGROWTHPRESS.COM

New Growth Press, Greensboro, NC 27404
www.newgrowthpress.com

Cover Design: Trish Mahoney, themahoney.com
Interior Typesetting and eBook: Lisa Parnell, lparnell.com

ISBN: 978-1-948130-32-5 (Print)
ISBN: 978-1-948130-33-2 (eBook)

Library of Congress Cataloging-in-Publication Data
Names: Fitzpatrick, Joel, 1977- author.
Title: Between us guys : life-changing conversations for dads and sons / Joel
  Fitzpatrick.
Description: Greensboro : New Growth Press, 2019.
Identifiers: LCCN 2018056267 (print) | LCCN 2019011379 (ebook) | ISBN
  9781948130332 (ebook) | ISBN 9781948130325 (trade paper)
Subjects: LCSH: Fathers and sons--Religious aspects--Christianity. | Child
  rearing--Religious aspects--Christianity. | Parenting--Religious
  aspects--Christianity.
Classification: LCC BV4529.17 (ebook) | LCC BV4529.17 .F58 2019 (print) | DDC
  248.8/421--dc23
LC record available at https://lccn.loc.gov/2018056267

Printed in The United States of America

26 25 24 23 22 21 20 19   2 3 4 5 6

To my wife, Ruth:
I love you deeply and am so thankful for you.

To my son, Colin:
Thank you for loving me, even though I fail you
so often. You are my favorite son.

To my daughter, Eowyn:
Thank you for giving me the space
to write this book. You are courageous, creative,
and my favorite daughter.

Contents

Introduction
Being a Man

Hi, Dad. I am happy that you have decided to pick up this book and join your son on a series of life-shaping discussions. This is a daunting task, I know. I have a son, and between his school, my work, and baseball practice, we are incredibly busy. Being a dad is not easy, and there are so many ways we are different from each other. But here are some things that I can guess about you:

- You love your son.
- You want to help him understand life.
- You live with low-level guilt, because you don't think you're doing enough to teach him about life.

I feel the exact same way. My son, Colin, is twelve years old now, and there are so many times I wish I could go back in time and have these formative conversations over again.

What you hold in your hands is my attempt at helping you have these conversations. Whether your son is older or younger, it is never too early or too late to start talking about what it means to be a man who loves God and his neighbor. If your son is older, tailor the questions and examples in this book so that they're more appropriate for his age.

WHAT IS A MAN? FOUR EXAMPLES

Read Matthew 19:13–15: "Then children were brought to him that he might lay his hands on them and pray. The disciples rebuked the people, but Jesus said, 'Let the little children come to me and do not hinder them, for to such belongs the kingdom of heaven.' And he laid his hands on them and went away."

The subject of "being a man" is such a touchy one that it's even hard to say. "Be a man" can cause so much hurt to those who don't fit into the typical models of what a man is. What does it mean to be a man? We have all kinds of ways that we think about how to answer this question. The entertainment industry seems to highlight three models of a man in particular: the weakling, the loser, and the womanizer.

Men come in all shapes and sizes. Men may even struggle with their manhood. So, what does it mean to be a man, and does the Bible hold out a clear description of a man? I think the answer is yes.

My dad, Phil, is a man—a manly man. But he is not the kind of man you normally expect to see when someone says, "Phil is a man." What makes him seem odd is that he loves children. For my entire life, my dad has been involved deeply in children's ministry. When kids squeal in delight, my dad squeals (literally) alongside them. It is his greatest joy in life to bring kids to Jesus and show them Jesus's love for them. When Dad walks into a room, his personality draws people to him in such a way that people walk away saying, "That is a man."

My father-in-law, George, is a man, too. He is a wise man. He is a wise counselor whom I go to when I don't know what to do next. He is a fierce teacher and counselor, incisive in his evaluation and biblical in his judgments. The thing that I love about him, too, is his attention to kids. When he walks into the room, he finds the children and takes an interest in them. He desires to make them feel known and loved.

I have another friend, Rip Pratt. He loves kids fiercely. He loves broken people fiercely. He loves Jesus. He is a youth pastor and has been one for the past thirty years. He loves to see kids exercise their God-given talents and abilities to serve others. He moves toward kids who may not fit into other youth groups; he loves them and then brings them to see Jesus.

One last friend is Wayne Houk Duguid. He is a man. He is a friend. He is a musician. He laughs uproariously. He sings loudly. He loves kids. He talks to my son and daughter as if they were his peers, not people who are too immature to be taken seriously. He loves Jesus, even though at times he struggles. He is not afraid to love. He is gentle, humble, and is going to hate me for writing these words about him. He doesn't need attention because he is settled in God's love for him, and he gives that love to my children.

These are four very different sorts of men, but when they are around me I know that there is something in them that causes me to say they are men. So why do I look at them and say, "These are men"?

The biblical view of manhood doesn't have to do with how a man talks, dresses, or his affinity for facial hair. A man is a broken, sinful person who looks to Christ for salvation, points others to Christ, and lays down his life so that others can live. A man understands that he cannot be good enough to earn God's love, and because of that he doesn't expect others to earn his. This manliness is put on display so beautifully in the image of God the Father, and it is lived out in families as dads try to live this way, and look to their good Father for acceptance and forgiveness. You get the opportunity to teach, train and instill this sort of lifestyle in your son. You get the cool responsibility of raising up your son to be a man who loves God and loves his neighbors—all through the vehicle of being a dad who has conversations about life with your son.

A DAD'S CALL

Dad, it can be really hard to know how to teach your son to be a man. But the Bible is clear on how you can teach your son: it says, *talk to him*. So, in our quest to learn how to speak to our sons, it will be helpful to look at three examples: Deuteronomy, Proverbs, and the apostle Paul.

- Deuteronomy 6:4–7 says, "Hear, O Israel: The Lord our God, the Lord is one. You shall love the Lord your God with all your heart and with all your soul and with all your might. And these words that I command you today shall be on your heart. You shall teach them diligently to your children, and shall talk of them when you sit in your house, and when you walk by the way, and when you lie down, and when you rise."
- Proverbs 1:8–9 says, "Hear, my son, your father's instruction, and forsake not your mother's teaching, for they are a graceful garland for your head and pendants for your neck."
- Ephesians 6:4 says, "Fathers, do not provoke your children to anger, but bring them up in the discipline and instruction of the Lord."

In all three of these verses, what do we read? As dads, we are given an amazing opportunity to be the primary influence for the gospel in our children's lives. But how do we do that? Look again at our three Scripture passages. We do it through conversations that happen in every area of our lives, encompassing every aspect of our lives.

This is not a book about how to make your son into a pious American Christian. This is a book about the only power in the universe who can cause us to love God and love our neighbor. If we fail to ground our sons in the finished work of Jesus for them, we will miss the point. The point of fatherhood is not just to make your kids obey. If that is the point, then you don't need a Christian book—you can go get a book written by anyone who'll give you practical advice. If our sons' hearts aren't changed by the gospel, then all we are doing is creating little Pharisees, whom Jesus called "whitewashed tombs" (Matthew 23:27).

We want our sons to know that God doesn't just save them and then expect them to earn their way into heaven. Yes, we will talk about what God calls us to do and who he calls us to be as followers of Christ, but that discussion will not take place outside of the context of the very thing that gives us the power to obey.

Hear this clearly. I know you may be tempted to ask, "Is Joel telling me that it doesn't matter if I sin or not? Is he telling me that it doesn't matter if my son is obedient?" (I know this because it is the temptation in my own heart.) So, here you go: Yes, you and your son need to obey. However, it is only Jesus's work for us that gives us the power to obey, and which brings meaning to our obedience.

A GUIDE AND A PERSONAL NOTE

What you have in your hands is a book full of conversations you can have with your sons. In fact, these chapters are written so that you can read them directly to your sons, if you choose. It includes conversations that cover so many different parts of life—money, friendship, sex, strength, defending others, and all sorts of other things. This list is by no means comprehensive, nor are these the only ways you can have these talks with your sons. What I hope to do is spark a lifetime of conversations that will build your relationship.

Take a second, pick up a highlighter, pen, or pencil, and look at the Table of Contents. Think and pray about your time with your sons, and then prioritize what topics you might want to cover first. You can go straight through the book or have the conversations piecemeal. The point of these conversations is that you have them, not the order in which you have them.

Each conversation has suggested questions that will help spur on conversation. If the question is directed toward your sons, it will say "Sons"; if it is for you to answer, it will say "Dads." The questions marked "Both" are for each of you to answer. Answer these questions truthfully, but don't feel the need to confess every sin you have ever committed. Use wisdom. Be transparent with your sons; show them you aren't perfect. It will go a long way toward encouraging your sons to be open and honest with you.

I love to have these conversations when I walk with my son at night during the week, when we are out fishing, or just when I am putting him to bed and he's had a tough day. Your mission, should you choose to accept it, is to try and make it natural. Yes, in the beginning it will feel forced; work through it. The rewards of being able to have fun, natural, and serious conversations all outweigh the risks of looking like a dork. (By the way, your son won't notice that you look like a dork; he will be happy that you're spending time together.)

It is important to say, though, that I don't have it all together. That makes writing this book scary. I am a sinner saved purely by the grace of God, and any wisdom I have comes directly from God's hand. Don't miss this; we are the same in this way. We are utterly dependent on God to be with us and to make these conversations worthwhile. So, let's get started in our talk *Between Us Guys*. I feel like a dork—do you? Let's do this together.

Talk 1
Our Friends

THEME: Men need friends. They need close relationships with other godly men who are wise, so that they live out to the fullest who God has made them to be.

GETTING TO JESUS: Jesus was the friend of sinners. He spent all his time with his friends, the disciples, building them up and caring for them. And now he is the friend who sticks closer than a brother (Proverbs 18:24; John 15:15).

SUGGESTED ACTIVITY: Take one of your son's friends from church with you guys today, and do something fun—maybe go out for a piece of pie or for a walk to the park where you can talk.

Imagine life without friends. It would be a pretty boring life. Sometimes we want to be alone, and that's good, but most of us want—and need—friends. It's hard to fit in, though, isn't it? A lot of the time finding friends is difficult. We may not look the same or like the same stuff.

WE WERE CREATED FOR THIS

SONS: Who are your friends? What do you like about them?

DADS: Who are your friends? What makes a good friend?

When God created Adam, he looked at Adam and saw that he was alone. God knew this was not good for Adam. So, what did he do? He created Eve. She was Adam's first friend. God did this because God is three persons who are all friends. God knows that friends bring out the best in us. They make us into the best, fullest men that we can be.

When we're around our friends, we find out more about ourselves. They laugh with us when we tell jokes. They help us when we are sad. We like when they are together with us. A good friend has your back, and you have theirs.

Friendships are where we learn how to live in community with other people. We learn how to like things that other people like. It is where we learn how to help people, where we learn how to share another person's pain. Friendships are so important.

Jesus had friends—the disciples, Mary, Martha, and others. But he had one friend, John, who was his closest earthly friend. John stuck with Jesus and Jesus loved John—so much so that when Jesus began the Lord's Supper (Communion), John was reclining at his side (John 13:23). There was physical closeness between the two of them, in a totally friendly way. Jesus loved John so much that when Jesus was dying, he asked John to care for his mother, and John accepted!

This is what friendship was always meant to be—people loving and serving each other, trying to meet their friend's needs. Friends can be so much fun and can point us to a better relationship. But the problem is that there are times when our friends fail us.

SIN HAS BROKEN US ALL

When our friends betray us, it is so hard, isn't it? Maybe it will happen when we tell a friend a secret, and he tells everyone. I can remember when I told a friend about something that was very secret; the next day, when I was with a different friend, he asked me about the secret. I was so embarrassed! I was hurt, and I struggled to trust friends anymore. We wonder what we did wrong to that friend to make them be so mean to us. We wonder if we will ever have true friends.

> **BOTH:** Have you ever been betrayed by a friend? What happened? Are you still friends?

When Adam and Eve sinned, they both betrayed their closest friends—God and each other. They turned their back on the friendship that they had with God and broke his trust; they didn't obey his law. And they betrayed their friendship with each other; they didn't protect each other, nor did they encourage each other to obey.

Friends can lead us in the right direction, but they can also lead us into sin. This is why choosing wise friends is so important. Friends have a lot of influence over us, so we need to find friends who will help us walk with God.

Read 1 Corinthians 15:33 (NIV): "Do not be misled: 'Bad company corrupts good character.'"

SONS: Have you ever had someone try to convince you to sin?

DADS: How have friends led you to sin in your past? (Share this story with your son. Spare the gory details, but it will help your son see that you are a sinner who needs Jesus, just like them.)

This is a huge problem for us. Now, because of sin, all of our relationships are broken. This brings sadness and frustration into our friendships. Sometimes our friends lie about us, take something of ours, or just ignore us, and we don't know why. Sometimes our friends become friends with other people, then leave us. This can be so frustrating. It can really hurt because you feel abandoned.

All of this is really hard—and it doesn't get easier as life goes on. Too many men give up on friendships because of these kinds of hurts or maybe because they think that friends are just too much work. But even though friendships are difficult and full of the pain of sin, Jesus redeems the pain of our friendships.

JESUS DIED TO MAKE IT BETTER

Did you know that Jesus was abandoned by his friends? When Jesus needed his friends the most, they all abandoned him and even denied being his friend.

Read Matthew 26:36–46 and Luke 22:54–62. Use the questions below or similar ones to discuss these passages with your son.

SONS: How did Jesus's friends betray him?

DADS: What do you think Jesus was feeling as his friends left him?

But here's the beauty of Jesus: he doesn't betray us. Jesus loved Peter so much that even though Peter denied Jesus three times, Jesus never stopped loving Peter! Jesus died for Peter—and for all of the disciples who abandoned him. There was nothing that the disciples could have done that would have stopped Jesus from being their friend.

Read Proverbs 18:24 (NIV): "One who has unreliable friends soon comes to ruin, but there is a friend who sticks closer than a brother."

You see, buddy, Jesus is just that good of a friend. He won't leave you, and he won't lead you to ruin; in fact, what he does is he calls us "friend." Jesus died to make things right, so that we can be friends with God.

Read John 15:15: "No longer do I call you servants, for the servant does not know what his master is doing; but I have called you friends."

This friendship changes everything for us.

HOW TO LIVE WITH LOVE

Jesus's friendship, his love for us, changes everything about us. When our friends betray us, we can know that Jesus never will. Jesus died to show us that he will stick with us forever! He is our friend, even when our friends leave us.

This does two things in us. First, it enables us to *be* good friends. We can learn from Jesus and stick with our friends, even when they do mean things to us. We sacrifice for our friends, even when they are selfish. We try and be good friends because we know that Jesus has forgiven us for all the times when we have been bad friends.

Second, it shows us what good friends look like so that we can choose the right kind of friends. The Bible is full of verses that talk about what a good friend is, but those qualities are sometimes difficult to see in a person. The best way to see what a good friend is, is to look at one. David and Jonathan were really good friends. They shared a love that was different than the love that happens even between a husband and wife. The Bible says, "The soul of Jonathan was knit to the soul of David, and Jonathan loved him as his own soul" (1 Samuel 18:1). Their affection for each other was based on deep friendship, love, and trust.

David and Jonathan had a friendship that was rooted in love—and it was a friendship that taught them what it meant to be men. Their friendship became the crown of their lives; they loved each other and would do anything for each other. It taught them humility while making each of them feel like they were worth loving. Their friendship led them to self-sacrifice, but they were repaid all that it took many times over. They walked side by side with each other through the difficulties of their lives.

You see, guys, friendship is very important. Too often, old men like me forget how important friends are. We forget to make friends and have deep friendships. Don't forget to make friends, keep friends, and to keep friendship a priority.

Talk 2
School, Work, and Our Identity

THEME: Oftentimes, we mix up our work with our identity. We find all our value as a man in the job that we perform. But Jesus has given us a new identity: an adopted son of the king.

GETTING TO JESUS: Jesus has called us to a vocation—a job—and it is good to work. But work is not our identity. Jesus gives us a new identity that marks us as different people.

SUGGESTED ACTIVITY: If you can schedule it, have this chapter's conversation over lunch on a work and/or school day. It will give both of you a nice break, and provide a visual representation of what it means to be someone who works.

Today we are going to talk about our work—and right now, for most boys, your work is school. Another word for that is "vocation." This is not a word we use all the time. Vocation is what God has made you to do. (We like to talk about vacation, but that's a very different thing.) Your vocation is what God has called you to do, right now, at this point in your life.

When someone says, "Tell me about yourself," what's the first thing you say? When you're a younger dude, you may say that you like to play baseball or something else. You may even say that you are a student. Now, ask a dad to tell you about himself. What does he say? He tells you about his work! He may say that he is a scientist or a garbageman; inevitably, the conversation will move to what he does for a living.

DADS: Why do you think we talk more about what we do than who we are?

WE WERE CREATED FOR THIS

Read Genesis 2:15: "The Lord God took the man and put him in the garden of Eden to work it and keep it."

When God made man, he told us a few things that we were created for, and one of those was work. Did you know that? We were created to work. That kind of sounds odd, doesn't it? Because work is not always fun or good; sometimes it is really difficult and takes a lot out of us.

DADS: What do you do for your work?

SONS: How is school your vocation?

God has called you to be like him, and for the first six days of creation, God worked. Then on the seventh day, he rested. So when we work, we are actually doing what God has created and called us to do. Adam and Eve were placed in the garden and told to work it. They were to water the plants, trim the trees, and guard the garden so that it would be a safe place. This means that work is good! It is good for us to be productive. It is good for you to learn.

SIN HAS BROKEN US ALL

But Adam and Eve sinned. They didn't do their jobs; they let Satan in, then he tempted them and they fell. And when Adam and Eve sinned, we all died spiritually. We were separated from God and became his enemies. This is a very sad and terrible place to be.

God sent Adam and Eve out of the garden—and from then on, work became difficult. It was no longer fun or easy to work on the plants in the garden. And today, we struggle at our work. It isn't easy to learn everything; sometimes it's hard. Sometimes people are mean to us, sometimes what we have to do is difficult, and sometimes we just plain fail.

DADS: What is the hardest thing you do at your work?

SONS: What is your hardest subject in school? Why?

School can become even more difficult. When we look at our grades and do good, we feel good about ourselves; if we do bad, we get angry with ourselves and feel like losers. We look at our school or our work to tell us who we are and if we are valuable.

But God still calls us to work. Dads (and moms) work to make money for the family to survive, to serve and love the community around them, and to fulfill what God has called them to do, to name just a few reasons. You go to school so that you can learn and grow. This is what God has called us to do; it is our vocation. But God has called us to so much more.

JESUS DIED TO MAKE IT BETTER

Before we become Christians, we are enemies of God, and we don't have his blessing on our vocations. But when we become Christians, Jesus gives us a new identity—he calls us brothers. Jesus brings us into the family of God through his work on the cross. The apostle Paul made this clear in his letters to the churches of his day. We don't work for this; we have been set free (Galatians 5:1). Jesus brings us into the family of God and makes us princes in his kingdom (Galatians 4:1–7). We are not given this new identity because we are good workers or because we obey all of God's commands. He does it by grace through faith, not by your works (Ephesians 2:8–9).

But even before he died, do you know what Jesus was doing? He was living; he was working. Can you believe it? Jesus went to school (Luke 2:46); he had to learn a trade; and he certainly must have had chores. What is amazing is that he never once complained about having to do work. He always did his chores and his "homework." And he did this so that when we do our school or housework and we complain, we still get Jesus's record of always doing his job perfectly.

This new identity that God gives us sets us free from having to look to our job, school, or even people's opinions of our work to feel like we are accepted. Do you know what this is like? When you don't do well on a test and fail or when you miss an important play in a game, you feel like a loser, like a failure. Those feelings are identity feelings—they say something about who you believe you are. But Jesus says that you are accepted, loved, cherished, and valuable, even when you get bad grades.

HOW WE LIVE WITH LOVE

Jesus saves us, gives us a new identity, and then gives us a job or a vocation to live out this new identity. When we read this, we usually only think about what job we're going to do. But in his letters, Paul wasn't talking just about our job as an engineer, a policeman, or a pastor. He was talking about our lives outside of work as well as our lives at work. Your vocation is what God has called you to do in the place you are. You are a student, a musician, a baseball player.

God tells us that we are his children and heirs of the kingdom. This means that whether you are a student or in the Army, both of those are callings that God has given to you. They are important because they're given by God.

Now, can you remember the second of the two great commandments? The first great commandment is to love the Lord your God with all your heart, soul, mind, and strength (Mark 12:30). Here is the second:

Read Matthew 22:39: "You shall love your neighbor as yourself."

When Jesus said this, he gave us a big piece of the puzzle for understanding how we should live out our vocation. God calls us to these various tasks so that we would show the love of God to our neighbors. So when you go to school, you study and you serve the other kids in your class as your way of loving your neighbor. You do your homework because that is your God-given task. You come home and serve your mother out of love; you do the dishes because that is your vocation.

Read Colossians 3:23–24: "Whatever you do, work heartily, as for the Lord and not for men, knowing that from the Lord you will receive the inheritance as your reward. You are serving the Lord Christ."

God calls us to our vocations. We do our good works for our neighbors, and when we work hard we are serving Jesus. We love others and serve them by holding out God's love to them. But so often we are lazy and don't carry out the good works God has set in front of us to do (Ephesians 2:10). It's at those moments when we fail—when we don't love God and our neighbor as we should in our vocations—that we need to remember that we have Christ's perfect righteousness. This gives us the hope and the strength to try to love again. This does not give you the right to go ahead and be a bum in your vocation; it gives you the strength to love, knowing that even if you fail, Jesus will forgive you!

Talk 3
Family

THEME: We have two families: our biological family and our church family. We are born into our biological family; Jesus brings us into our new church family through his sacrifice.

GETTING TO JESUS: Jesus has brought us into a new family, making us his brothers. Because of that work, we can love both our biological family and our church family with generosity.

SUGGESTED ACTIVITY: Go grab some frozen yogurt and pile on the toppings. In an odd way, this good, sweet treat is a picture of the blessings that we have by being in God's family. Enjoy!

Today on our walk, we are going to spend some time talking about our two families. Did you know that you have two families? Can you guess who they are? God has given us both our biological families and our church families, to help us understand God's care for us, how authority is good for us, and that God accepts us because he loves us. Sometimes we experience these truths because our two families act kindly, and sometimes we begin to understand them through the hard times, mistakes, and sin (ours and others).

> **BOTH:** What do you like most about our family?

WE WERE CREATED FOR THIS

> **SONS:** Do you know that I love you? (Hopefully your son will answer "yes." If not, then you need to assure him of your love.) Why do you think I love you?

I love you so much; you are my boy, and we are family. When God created the world, he looked at Adam and knew that it was not good for him to be alone, so he made Eve. God put Adam and Eve together and they had children, because God knew that it was good for them to be together. God knew that children could not survive on their own, so he gave them parents. God knew that parents would come to know more about him by being parents, so he gave Adam and Eve children.

God even knew how much parents would love and enjoy their children, just like God loves and enjoys us, so he gave me you. God did all of this so that you would know him and understand that he loves you.

DADS: Why is it good for us to be a family?

SONS: What would life be like if we didn't have a family? What would life be like if we were abandoned by our parents?

God gave us each other to love and protect each other. Family is so important. The Bible is the story of how God worked through one family to make a new, much larger family. It is the story of how God called Abraham to leave his homeland to go to a new land, and how God protected Abraham and his descendants to bring us Jesus, who would make us into a new kind of people. The people of Israel were related by blood; Christians are a spiritual family.

So let's talk about our biological family first. God has given us a biological family of mom, me, sister, grandma, grandpa, aunts, uncles, cousins, etc. He gives us each other as good gifts so that we can learn to love people and receive their love. God gives us dads and moms so that we can learn about who God is and how we relate to each other. God has given us each other to show his love for us and to help us learn to love each other. Our biological family is where we learn how to live in this world.

But God doesn't just give us our biological family to teach us his love for us. When we become Christians, he gives us another much bigger family. He gives us our church family, called the body of Christ. We are adopted by God the Father and brought into this new family. What makes us part of God's family is not our last name or our genes; it's the Holy Spirit. When we are in God's family, God never loves us more or less than other Christians. He never loves us more because we act good or less because we act bad. God the Father treats us like he treats Jesus. Being a part of this family means that God is with us and will bring us to be with him when we die.

SIN HAS BROKEN US ALL

But our family doesn't always get along, do we? Sometimes your brother or sister does something to annoy you. Sometimes you disobey me or your mother. When we do these things to each other, we can get angry and sin against each other. We still love our family, even when we are really mad at them, but sometimes we still do things that we know will make our family members angry.

Sin tries to break the relationships that we share with each other. It makes us think that our family members don't love us. Sin breaks everything, and the thing is, all of us sin against each other.

DADS: What is the thing you struggle with most in your family? Are you ever mean to your brother or sister? Are they ever mean to you?

SONS: What are some of the things that you think are broken about our family?

Just like our families, churches can be broken with sin. People can say things that are mean; pastors can sin against the people in their church. Just like a biological family, we love each other, but our sins can break our relationships with the other people in the church. Sin makes things difficult in a church. It can even make it difficult to want to go to church or to be involved in relationships within the church.

Here is the problem: our church family is meant to be made up of people who love and accept us for who we are, but often they sin against us. Even worse than that, we also sin against others. This sad reality causes pain and heartache right in the place where we should find healing and rest.

JESUS DIED TO MAKE IT BETTER

Jesus is so kind. He didn't leave us to live with our families who are full of sin and brokenness; he died to forgive us for the ways we sin against our family and then he brings us into a forever family. You see, every time we sin before we are Christians, our sin separates us from God our Father. But Jesus died so that we would be adopted into a new family. Jesus said something kind of odd in Matthew 19:29.

Read Matthew 19:29: "And everyone who has left houses or brothers or sisters or father or mother or children or lands, for my name's sake, will receive a hundredfold and will inherit eternal life."

Jesus was talking to his disciples about the reality that, at times, it feels like we lose out on stuff when we follow him, and that is true. It is costly to follow Jesus. For the people he was talking to, it would cost them relationships, money, possessions, and maybe even their lives. But Jesus promised that when they followed him they would gain back so much more—even eternal life.

Read Romans 8:15–17: "For you did not receive the spirit of slavery to fall back into fear, but you have received the Spirit of adoption as sons, by whom we cry, 'Abba, Father!' The Spirit himself bears witness with our spirit that we are children of God, and if children, then heirs—heirs of God and fellow heirs with Christ, provided we suffer with him in order that we may also be glorified with him."

> **BOTH:** Who do you know who is adopted? Talk about that family.

When we put our faith in Jesus and he saves us, he gives us a gift that brings us into a new family. Can you guess what that gift is? (Answer: the Spirit of God.) When we have the Spirit of God in us, we are adopted into God's family. We become his sons, and he becomes our Father. But notice what this passage says about how we are seen by God. God sees us as heirs and fellow heirs with Christ. Do you know what that means?

> **DADS**: What does it mean to be an heir?
>
> **SONS**: What are the kinds of things that we inherit from God?

When we are fellow heirs with Jesus, all the good things that Jesus earned by living the perfect life are saved for us too. He protects that inheritance and is saving it for when we get to heaven to be with him.

HOW WE LIVE WITH LOVE

God doesn't only want you to learn about what to believe about him and how to love him; he also wants us to learn what it means to live under authority. Let's think about the fifth commandment. Do you remember what it is?

Read Exodus 20:12: "Honor your father and your mother, that your days may be long in the land that the LORD your God is giving you."

Read Ephesians 6:1–3: "Children, obey your parents in the Lord, for this is right. 'Honor your father and mother' (this is the first commandment with a promise), 'that it may go well with you and that you may live long in the land.'"

But do you know that God talks to me as your dad as well? Listen to what God says right after Ephesians 6:1–3.

Read Ephesians 6:4: "Fathers, do not provoke your children to anger, but bring them up in the discipline and instruction of the Lord."

God desires that I love you and teach you—that I don't make you angry unnecessarily ("provoke") you, but that I bring you up. You know what's kind of funny? That's what we're doing right now. One day you may be a dad, and this is the life that you should lead with your child too.

This is what makes me so happy to be a part of this family—when God adopts you, he is the one who keeps you in his family. God is not a father like I am—when you disobey me, at times I get angry. But when we sin against God, he doesn't get angry with us; he disciplines us out of love for us. And there is nothing that we can do to break his love for us. Even when we sin, he forgives us and continues to love us with his everlasting love.

Family is one of the places where we can not only learn about love but also frequently practice forgiveness. We tend to sin against our family members more than anyone else, because they are so close to us. Our family relationships are primary places for us to practice the same forgiveness Jesus has demonstrated to us. When we let go of the offenses committed against us, we show our brother, sister, or parent that we understand we are also sinners and are also dependent upon Jesus for grace and forgiveness.

God is never ashamed that we are his sons. He loves us so much that he gave Jesus so that we could be a part of his family—and if he would not spare Jesus for us, how will he keep any of his love and good things from us?

Talk 4
Our Play

THEME: Hobbies and play are important parts of what it means to be men. They build friendships, help us develop new skills, and provide the rest that we need.

GETTING TO JESUS: Jesus gave us creativity, and gives us the space to play and have hobbies.

SUGGESTED ACTIVITY: If you are into it, do some woodworking. Build a bench for the house. It's fun and allows you to do some "manly" stuff with "manly" tools. Or choose some other creative activity that you and your son enjoy doing together. If you don't have any activity like that, now is a great time to come up with one!

God loves beautiful things. He is so creative. He also loves funny things. When I look at some of the creatures that God has made, I cannot help but think that God has a sense of humor. Especially the platypus—those things look weird.

When I think about how different animals act when they are in groups, I cannot help but think that God loves play. Especially dolphins: I love how they jump and flop and fly and spin out of the water, all to the glory of God. Think about it: animals play all over the place. Dogs play, cats play, horses play, lions play, and on and on.

WE WERE CREATED FOR THIS

We too love to play. In every culture, at almost every stage of life, humans play. They play games, play tricks, play sports—we all like to play. We play with our friends, our parents, people we don't know, and babies. I mean, have you ever seen a big, strong, burly man around a cute baby who's in a playful mood? What does he do? He plays and makes funny noises.

Playing does something in us. It gives us space to be serious and competitive. Games can change the most calm, sweet person and bring out their competitive side. It allows us to let our guard down so that we laugh uproariously and squeal with delight. We yell at each other and get mad when we lose; we gloat when we win. We have space to let a side of us show that often gets hidden when we are at school or work.

BOTH: What's your favorite game?

DADS: Did you play sports when you were younger? Did you like them? What did you like most about them?

Playing is less about doing a task and more about being a whole person. Playing is not about working; it is about resting (even though after you play, you're stimulated and possibly exhausted). When we play basketball, we want to score, but we also want to have fun and enjoy the process of dribbling and shooting. When we put together a new Lego set, we don't just want one big piece that is already assembled; we want to put it together. We enjoy the process, the accomplishment, and the friendships that we build as we play together.

SIN HAS BROKEN US ALL

Here is the problem, though: when we play and we lose, we can get angry. We can yell at our teammates, throw the video-game controller, or just be plain grumpy when our Legos don't fit together the way we want them to. We struggle with losing, we get frustrated when we don't catch a fish, and in one sense this is good because it makes us work hard.

But when we get angry either at our friends or at God for things not turning out the way we want, we sin. This sin breaks relationships and makes playing no fun. We get angry because we think we are the best, or think our friends have failed us. But what is behind all that anger is a lack of trust for God and what he has planned for us. Our anger and jealousy turn enjoyment, fulfillment, and fun into distrust of our friends and a desire to be better than everyone else.

We want what we want and get angry if we don't get it. This is why there is such a thing as a "rage quit"; we get so angry that we quit the video game or take our hammer and hit the piece of wood. We blame everyone and everything around us in our frustration.

> **DADS**: When did you get the angriest because you lost or because a fun day didn't turn out the way you wanted?
>
> **SONS**: How does losing make you feel? Why?

JESUS DIED TO MAKE IT BETTER

It may seem weird that Jesus would live and die so that we could experience playing and hobbies. It may even seem like a bit of a stretch to say that Jesus liked to smile, play, and have fun. This is hard because there is not a single story of Jesus messing around in the Bible. In fact, the picture of Jesus we think we see in the New Testament is of a guy who is super serious all the time. So how does the gospel transform the way we play?

Let's think about what we know about God and man. God created everything, including the animals that we see jumping and spinning, the dogs we see running. That same God made man in his image. Humans are creative, and we love to play! When God made us in his image, he didn't make humans to be his twins, but he did make us so that we would be like him. He created us to rule, to be just, to be holy, and yes, even to be creative.

DADS: What does it mean that we are created in God's image? Does that mean that we look like God, or that we share some of the same characteristics as God?

SONS: If we are made in the image of God and we love to play, does God care about playing?

Here is something we don't usually think about too often: Jesus was a boy, and he grew up in a family with siblings, and he had friends. What do we know about young kids? They like to play!

Now here is the coolest thing ever: we know Jesus never sinned and that he never was a sinner. He never got angry because he lost. He never put off his work in disobedience in order to play. Jesus probably liked to play and was a close friend to his disciples. And while we don't have a story of Jesus telling a joke or playing a game or even having a hobby, we do know how we are—and it would be hard to think that the creator of play would not play. The creator of wood then took that wood and made a bench. It is hard to think that he would not have used his creativity to make something beautiful.

Jesus did this without complaint, without sin, without getting angry if things didn't go his way. Then Jesus died and took all of the punishment for the times that *we* sin when we play. Every time you deserve to be punished for being proud and gloating over the losing team. Every time you get frustrated because something you are building doesn't turn out right and you break it. Every time you quit a game in rage and deserve punishment for your anger, Jesus took that punishment for you! That is good news. He did it because he chose to love you and to die for you.

> **SONS:** What would it be like if, when you played, no one ever got angry at a loss?
>
> **DADS:** What is it like to know that you are completely forgiven for all the times you got angry when you were playing, or worked on your hobby and got angry because it didn't go your way?

HOW WE LIVE WITH LOVE

Jesus loves it that we are creatures that find joy in our play and creativity. He loves our play and hobbies because when we do those things, we are acting like him. Isn't that fun! You see, we live with love by enjoying play, by having a hobby making fun things.

Hobbies can be all sorts of things, from playing golf to woodworking to making knives to singing or playing an instrument. Hobbies allow us the space to exercise our brains to accomplish a goal while having a fun, relaxing time. You see, the only point of learning to play the banjo is to play music. The only point of building a bench, as a hobby, is to rest on it.

When we don't get what we want when we want it, that is a very good thing. God is building character in us as we have to work hard and take our time to build. When we do this, we can act like God, who is a creator. We can understand in part what God meant when he stood back and looked at his creation and called it good. We can participate in the world, adding to its beauty by what we make, shape, and form with our hands and our minds.

God values this sort of creativity, and he showed it when the temple was built. Second Chronicles 2 tells us about all the people who were brought in from all over the place to help build the temple. What God was interested in were people who knew how to work to make things beautiful. That does not mean that to be accepted by God we need to be able to work with wood, but it does mean that God values our creativity. And while we are not called to use our talents to build a temple, we can use our talents to create beauty, and God may allow us to use our talents to serve his church. Whether we use woodworking to build a communion table, learn to play an instrument to help lead the people of God in worship, or just play a game with the other kids at church, in all these things we can love God and love our neighbor.

BOTH: Discuss some hobbies that you might want to take up together.

Talk 5
Love

THEME: God tells us to love him and to love our neighbor, but this is really hard.

GETTING TO JESUS: Jesus is the one who loved perfectly and gives us freedom to love God and share his love with others.

SUGGESTED ACTIVITY: Plan a trip where you can serve others—such as a person in your church who needs a visit, a food bank, or a homeless shelter. Take your son to a place where he will have a chance to serve others and show the love of God to them.

Today we are going to practice loving people. Do you remember the two greatest commandments?

Read Matthew 22:36–40: "'Teacher, which is the great commandment in the Law?' And he said to him, 'You shall love the Lord your God with all your heart and with all your soul and with all your mind. This is the great and first commandment. And a second is like it: You shall love your neighbor as yourself. On these two commandments depend all the Law and the Prophets.'"

Read the Ten Commandments (Exodus 20:2–17).

> **SONS:** Who do we love in the first four commandments? Who do we love in the last six commandments?

WE WERE CREATED FOR THIS

See, buddy, we were created to love God and love our neighbor. When God created Adam and Eve, he told them how to love each other and how to love him. God loved them, and they loved him back. It was beautiful.

We were created to love God. God loved to walk in the garden with Adam and Eve; he desired that they love him. But he also wanted them to love each other, because when they lived with love they would be like him. When we love God and others, we are living the way we were created to live.

SIN HAS BROKEN US ALL

When Satan came to Adam and Eve in the garden, he gave Adam and Eve a choice: love and trust God, or love yourself. Adam and Eve chose to love themselves—to give up the good relationship they had with God and instead trade it for what they wanted.

Remember Jesus's words we just read—that we are to love God with everything we are? That means God requires us to love him with every thought, every word, and every deed. Then he tells us to love our neighbors the way that we love ourselves.

BOTH: How are you doing at keeping God's commandments? What are some of the ways you struggle to love God and your neighbor?

You see, sin has come in and has made it so that we cannot love the way that we are supposed to love. Sin breaks our love.

JESUS DIED TO MAKE IT BETTER

The only person who was able to love the way God wants us to love is Jesus. Jesus knew loving God meant obeying his commands at all times, even when he knew it would be difficult. Jesus always obeyed God. In the garden of Gethsemane, Jesus faced one of his toughest tests. He knew that to obey God the Father out of love, he would have to suffer and die. But he loved God the Father so much he obeyed.

Read Luke 22:42: "Father, if you are willing, remove this cup from me. Nevertheless, not my will, but yours, be done."

Read John 15:12–14: "This is my commandment, that you love one another as I have loved you. Greater love has no one than this, that someone lay down his life for his friends. You are my friends if you do what I command you."

This is what is so amazing about Jesus; he committed the greatest act of love for us. He loved us so much that he would even love his enemies.

Read Romans 5:8: "But God shows his love for us in that while we were still sinners, Christ died for us."

HOW WE LIVE WITH LOVE

So, how do we live with love? All through the New Testament we read that our love should be given to our neighbors. Our loving obedience is lived out with the people who God brings into our lives.

Read Luke 10:25–37.

Jesus knew that we would ask the question, "Who is my neighbor?" In this parable we find out that our neighbors are even those people who are our enemies. God wants us to live with love for our families, our churches, and even our enemies. We are not supposed to just walk by people who are poor; we are to love them and serve them.

But the problem is that we struggle to love in this way. This is why we need Jesus so much. Jesus loves us so much that he takes away all the sin of not loving others, and gives us his perfect record of loving all the time perfectly. Because Jesus loved us that way, his love should make us want to love God and then our neighbor.

Jesus not only gives us his record of loving; he also gives us the power to love. When Jesus died, he promised to send his Spirit to give us the power we need to be able to live for him (John 16:7–14). The Spirit was his gift of love for us. This is why we need the love of Jesus so badly. Without Jesus, without the Holy Spirit, we would be left to our own power to love others. The Holy Spirit keeps making us into people who love like our Savior. Jesus loves us so much that he never leaves us.

BOTH: Think of some ways you can spend time loving your neighbor together, then plan a time to do it.

Talk 6
Generosity

THEME: Jesus wants us to be generous with all of the good things he has given us so that we can look like him.

GETTING TO JESUS: The only reason we can become generous is because Jesus was generous to us.

SUGGESTED ACTIVITY: Before this talk, go volunteer at a local homeless food distribution. Or make a meal for a needy family in your neighborhood or church. Or put together a care package for a homeless person you might see (you can keep it in your car so it's handy). Brainstorm with your son some useful items for this package. After you're done, go out for dinner. It will be good for you and your son to be hungry so that you experience the hunger that the poor face all day. Enjoy a dessert if you have time, as a sweet treat.

Do you remember us telling you, over and over, to share your toys? Your brother or sister would come and take your action figure or your Legos and you would go ballistic trying to get them back. You had your stuff, and you didn't want anyone else to have it. When we tried to help you share, we were trying to teach you that generosity was important.

> **BOTH:** Describe generosity. Think of words, phrases, or people, and write them down. See if your answers are changed at all by the end of this talk.

What we want to do on this walk is talk about generosity and hopefully be encouraged to share not only our toys or our money (that's the easy stuff), but to share our time, love, homes, and forgiveness with the people around us. True generosity is much harder than you think, so we want to be sure to talk about Jesus as well—because without him, we can't be the generous people we should be.

WE WERE CREATED FOR THIS

"Sharing is caring" is an old saying that people used to say a bunch, and it's true: when you share, you show that you care for the people around you. You show that you care for someone when you share with them what's valuable to you. You bring them into your life and give them the ability to take what you love and either make it their own or break it. It's kind of scary.

But generosity doesn't just have to do with toys, food, or physical things—because generosity didn't just start when the world was created. It started much earlier than that. It started with God. God has always been generous. We know that there are three persons in God—who are they? The Father, Son, and Holy Spirit. And they have existed, generously giving to each other for eternity. Think about that for a minute. God has always been a generous God, and he has always loved and enjoyed sharing himself with the other people in the Trinity—the Father always loving the Son, the Son always loving the Spirit.

We were created to be generous, because we were created to be like God. That is why, when we share we care, because when we share we are being the people God made us to be. When we are generous we are being like God, who was so generous with us, sacrificing his own life for us so that we can be rich with his grace, love, and eternal life.

Read 2 Corinthians 8:9: "For you know the grace of our Lord Jesus Christ, that though he was rich, yet for your sake he became poor, so that you by his poverty might become rich."

SONS: What would it be like if your friends were generous with all of their toys and all of their friendships?

DADS: How hard is it to be generous with people you love?

Again, generosity is not just about our toys, food, and money—it is about our love, forgiveness, time, friendship, and so much more. You see, God didn't just stop at giving Adam and Eve food and toys; he gave them a home to live, where God was. In fact, God walked with Adam in the afternoon (Genesis 3:8); he took Adam and shared his desires with him, telling Adam what he wanted and how he wanted Adam to have all that he needed. God was incredibly generous to Adam and Eve.

Read Genesis 1:28–30; 2:15–25.

SIN HAS BROKEN US ALL

But Satan is sneaky. He didn't show up and say, "Hey, I am Satan, and I am here to ruin your life and the lives of everyone who will come after you. Wanna hear how?" What he did was attack the goodness and generosity of God. He called God a liar and accused him of holding out on Adam and Eve. "Did God actually say . . . ?"; "You will not surely die. For God knows that when you eat of it your eyes will be opened, and you will be like God, knowing good and evil" (Genesis 3:1, 4–5).

Eve was tricked; she believed Satan's lie. Adam believed Satan, and stood by and let it all happen. And now, our generosity bone is broken. Instead of trusting in God's generosity to them, Adam and Eve decided to take what they wanted. They took what God had commanded them not to take; they ate what God had commanded them not to eat; and because of that, we struggle to trust another person's generosity and struggle to give up what we have.

Sin has broken our ability to give our love fully. It is hard to love people who sin against you. When your sister or brother takes your stuff when you ask them not to, it is hard to love them. Sin has broken our ability to forgive each other. When I get angry with you and sin against you, it is hard for you to forgive me.

> **SONS:** What would it be like to be generous with your enemies?
>
> **DADS:** Why is it so difficult for us to be generous with people who sin against us?

JESUS DIED TO MAKE IT BETTER

But in the middle of all those hard times, when we don't want to be generous with the people around us, Jesus is still generous with us. The Bible tells us about the generosity of Jesus.

Read Philippians 2:5–8: "Have this mind among yourselves, which is yours in Christ Jesus, who, though he was in the form of God, did not count equality with God a thing to be grasped, but emptied himself, by taking the form of a servant, being born in the likeness of men. And being found in human form, he humbled himself by becoming obedient to the point of death, even death on a cross."

Jesus gave up his riches. He set them aside to become a human and to serve humanity by living the life we needed to live, dying the death we deserved, and then being raised again. And here is the beauty of that: he didn't take the credit for doing that and keep his riches for himself—no, because he is generous, he has made us princes in God's kingdom, and we get to share in Jesus's inheritance.

Read Ephesians 2:4–7: "But God, being rich in mercy, because of the great love with which he loved us, even when we were dead in our trespasses, made us alive together with Christ—by grace you have been saved—and raised us up with him and seated us with him in the heavenly places in Christ Jesus, so that in the coming ages he might show the immeasurable riches of his grace in kindness toward us in Christ Jesus."

HOW WE LIVE WITH LOVE

Here is the hard part: we show the love that God has given us by being generous with other people. We give because we have been given to. But it still can be hard, because we don't believe that God has already given us everything that we need and won't stop being generous with us.

I love cookies. If I found the best cookie in the world but there was only one, would I be generous with that cookie? Well, maybe with those people whom I love, but most likely not. Would I be generous with my enemies? Definitely not. But if I knew that I had an unlimited supply of those cookies, and the cookie maker had promised me that he would make me the cookies any time I needed them, would I be generous then? Yeah!

Now, the final layer: What if I had been really mean to the cookie maker before he gave me his promise, but he gave me his promise anyway? Would I be willing to give cookies to my enemies? I think so.

This is how we live with love. We live generously with the people around us, because God has been so generous with us. We know that God has given us everything we need "according to his riches in glory"

(Philippians 4:19). Because God has promised to be generous with us so that we will have what we need, we can be generous with others.

Talk 7
Failure and Perfection

THEME: Jesus knows we are not perfect. He knows we will fail to obey, to be kind, and even to remember him at times. But he loves us in our failure and gives us the strength to obey.

GETTING TO JESUS: Jesus was perfect in our place, to release us from the pressure of having to be perfect.

SUGGESTED ACTIVITY: Do something that will challenge your son—something he will struggle with. Then take him out for ice cream.

Do you like to fail? Do you enjoy making all kinds of mistakes when you're working on a project? How about losing the game for your team—is that fun? No! We all want to be the best at what we do. No one wants to fail. But the funny thing is that we always expect to be perfect, so then when we fail we can't stand it!

DADS: When was the last time you got frustrated because you were not perfect at your job? What kind of emotions did you experience?

SONS: What types of emotions do you experience when you are not perfect at something that means a lot to you?

WE WERE CREATED FOR THIS

Isn't that weird? We know that we aren't perfect—experience tells us that—but we still expect perfection from ourselves. That is kind of freaky, but it tells us something important about ourselves: we were created for something more than failure. We long for success. We long for perfection because perfection is how we were created and what we will be recreated to be.

When Adam and Eve were created, they were placed in the garden and it was perfect. Perfect weather, perfect animals, perfect grass, perfect fruit, perfect trees, and on and on. But that is not all—their relationship was perfect. Adam and Eve never fought, never wished the other person would do more for them. They experienced perfection.

BOTH: Talk for a minute about what it would be like if everything you did turned out right. How would that make you feel? What would you do? What would you eat? What game would you play?

When Adam and Eve planted a garden, it always produced fruits and vegetables. When they learned something new, they never failed to remember it. When God told them to obey, they never disobeyed. They never felt the shame of having to face the reality that they weren't good enough. And if they would have continued to obey, we too would know what that is like.

Read Genesis 1:31: "And God saw everything that he had made, and behold, it was very good."

SIN HAS BROKEN US ALL

But then, it happened. Adam and Eve were tempted by Satan, and they failed. Perfection was lost, and today we all struggle with failure. While Adam and Eve could have obeyed, kept the law, and won for all the human race, they failed, they sinned, and everyone since then has lived under the terrible pressure of knowing they should be perfect and yet are never able to be.

There is an old myth about a guy called Sisyphus. That's a funny name, isn't it? Try saying it three times fast; I'll bet you can't do it perfectly. According to the myth, Sisyphus was a king who tried to trick the Greek god Zeus and failed. His punishment was to roll a huge rock up a large hill. When he got to the top, the rock would roll back down the hill, and he would have to start all over again.

This is kind of like our desire to be perfect. It makes life absurd, crazy, frustrating, and sad. We try our hardest to do the right thing, and yet there is no one who is perfect (Romans 3:10–18). No one can even come close, because the Bible tells us that all the desires of our hearts are bent toward evil and are tainted with sin all the time (Genesis 6:5). Even when we want to do good, we end up doing the things that we don't want to do, and when we want to do good, we do the exact opposite.

This is really bad news. In fact, the apostle Paul was thinking about this in Romans 7, and at the end of the chapter he asked this amazing question: If it is true that I will never be perfect, then who will save me?

Read Romans 7:15, 18–19, 24:

> For I do not understand my own actions. For I do not do what I want, but I do the very thing I hate. . . . For I know that nothing good dwells in me, that is, in my flesh. For I have the desire to do what is right, but not the ability to carry it out. For I do not do the good I want, but the evil I do not want is what I keep on doing. . . . Wretched man that I am! Who will deliver me from this body of death?

BOTH: Discuss the areas in both of your lives where you want to do better. It can be school, work, following Christ, loving others. (Dads, this is a good chance to identify with your son as he struggles.)

JESUS DIED TO MAKE IT BETTER

Here is the beautiful thing about Romans 7, though: it doesn't end with that question. God doesn't leave Christians in their failure, frustration, and shame. Paul asked in frustration, "Who will deliver me from this body of death?" In other words: Who will rescue me from myself? Who will make things better? God is so kind to put this question here. You see, he doesn't expect you to be perfect. In fact, he knows that you won't be!

God answered Paul's question. Let's pick up where we left off.

Read Romans 7:24–8:4:

Wretched man that I am! Who will deliver me from this body of death? Thanks be to God through Jesus Christ our Lord! So then, I myself serve the law of God with my mind, but with my flesh I serve the law of sin. There is therefore now no condemnation for those who are in Christ Jesus. For the law of the Spirit of life has set you free in Christ Jesus from the law of sin and death. For God has done what the law, weakened by the flesh, could not do. By sending his own Son in the likeness of sinful flesh and for sin, he condemned sin in the flesh, in order that the righteous requirement of the law might be fulfilled in us, who walk not according to the flesh but according to the Spirit.

I know that was not the easiest part of the Bible to understand, but let's look at it for a second. God knows that we have to be perfect to earn his love. He also knows that we can't be perfect. We too know that we can't be perfect, and that frustrates us. So, God came down to earth and became a man to be perfect for us! God the Father sent Jesus the Son to be the person we need to be to earn God the Father's love for us!

Here is the point: Jesus was perfect so that you don't have to be. You don't have to be perfect in sports, school, fishing, lawn mowing, or Lego-building for God your Father to love and accept you. The pressure is off. You don't have to be perfect to keep God happy with you, to keep God loving you. Jesus was perfect for you! This means that when you miss a long spot while mowing the lawn and the grass has a mohawk, you aren't a failure. When you mess up and get angry, God doesn't get angry at you! You can admit that you aren't perfect, and yet know that you are loved so deeply that you will never break that love.

I can hear you asking the million-dollar question: what makes us want to obey God, then? Just hold on and let me work on that next.

HOW WE LIVE WITH LOVE

When you get a really good gift from someone and you don't deserve that gift—in fact, you deserve to be punished, but you get a gift instead—how do you respond to the gift-giver? Do want to punch him or her in the face? No, of course not! Do you want to go around talking bad about the gift-giver? No! You want to tell people how generous he or she is, right?

You see, when you are freed from the pressure of being perfect because you have been given the gift of Jesus's perfection, it doesn't make you want to live like a crazy person—it makes you want to tell people about that amazing gift! It makes you want to follow after Jesus, not your desire to sin. This is the way the gospel works. As we think about what Jesus has done and we read what he wants us to do, we fall in love with him and want to live the way he wants us to live. We don't beat ourselves or others up because we can't be perfect. Instead we live with forgiveness, understanding, and love.

Read 2 Corinthians 3:17: "Now the Lord is the Spirit, and where the Spirit of the Lord is, there is freedom."

The freedom that God gives us is the freedom to try and obey without the pressure of being perfect or the fear of failure. God knows that you're not perfect. Jesus knows you will fail, yet he loves you. You are secure in his love. It is kind of like you're playing a game and your team has already won. Now, you just have to play the game with freedom.

BOTH: What would it be like if you lived like you were free from trying to be perfect—if you knew you were accepted and loved, imperfections and all?

Talk 8
Disappointment

THEME: When we are disappointed by what happens today, we can trust that Jesus's plan for us is good and will turn out for our good.

GETTING TO JESUS: Jesus knew what it was like to face disappointment, and he overcame it to give us hope.

SUGGESTED ACTIVITY: Go for a walk, especially if your son has lost a game recently, gotten a bad grade on a test, or had a friendship fall apart.

Can you think of a time when you were really disappointed? I can remember when I worked really hard studying for a test, and when I took it I thought I got an A for sure. But when I got the test back, it turned out that I'd gotten a C; I had read the test wrong, and answered the questions the wrong way. I was super-frustrated—all that work down the drain!

Another time I was coaching my son's baseball team and we made it all the way to the city championships. We thought that we were the best team in our league, but the day when we played the game, we lost.

The whole team was disappointed; we had worked for months to win that game, and we lost.

Disappointment happens to all of us. Sometimes we want something so bad, we work and work to get it, but we fail to get it. Or even worse: Have you ever gotten what you wanted and then it ended up not meeting your expectations? That's the worst.

WE WERE CREATED FOR THIS

SONS: Have you ever done really good at school? What did it feel like?

BOTH: Talk about a time when you were really disappointed.

I don't think I have ever met a person who loves to be disappointed. Why? Why is it that we all hate to be disappointed?

It is because we were created to be satisfied. In our relationships and with our things, we were created to be satisfied. God created Adam and Eve and set them in the garden. And when he created them, they were holy and happy; they had everything they needed. They were together and never disappointed each other. They knew what it was like to always be fulfilled. Wow, what an amazing thing!

> **BOTH:** What would it be like if you always had what you needed/wanted when you needed/wanted it, and were never disappointed? What if you and your friends always lived to please the other person?

This is what we were created for—joy and fulfillment all the time in our relationships, in our things, and in God.

SIN HAS BROKEN US ALL

But as with all things, Adam and Eve were tricked to think that what they had was not enough. Satan came into the garden and lied to Adam and Eve; he told them that God was holding out on them and that they could find satisfaction by going outside his plan. But the funny thing is, God never holds out on us. He always gives us more than we could ever imagine.

Adam and Eve believed the lie and gave up satisfaction with God for disappointment without God. Now, we all suffer. We all want to have something more, and we are never satisfied; in fact, we are constantly disappointed. Nothing ever gives us the complete satisfaction we are looking for. Everyone's life shows this. When we get one thing, we want another. I mean, how many Legos can one person own? Yet, when a new set comes out, we want that one. When we make friends, we fight. When we love people, we disappoint them. We don't do what they want us to do; we aren't who they want us to be. We all struggle, we all sin—especially when we don't get what we want when we want it, in the way we want to get it!

> **SONS**: What are some of the feelings you have when you don't get what you want or when a big plan falls apart?

Read James 4:1–2: "What causes quarrels and what causes fights among you? Is it not this, that your passions are at war within you? You desire and do not have, so you murder. You covet and cannot obtain, so you fight and quarrel. You do not have, because you do not ask."

What is Jesus's brother James saying? He is saying that the reason we struggle with disappointment is because we want things. They could be good things, like food or friendship or exciting experiences, or they could be bad things. Either way, we want them. We demand that other people give them to us. When people don't give us what we want, we become angry and disappointed with them. This happens to all of us.

> **DADS**: When you were a boy, what did you really want that you didn't get? What did you want to accomplish that you didn't accomplish? How did that make you feel?

JESUS DIED TO MAKE IT BETTER

Here is the good news: even though we get disappointed and angry with people who don't give us what we want, God has given us everything we need. He does that through Jesus. You see, Jesus faced disappointment. He was in the garden of Gethsemane and asked his disciples to pray with him, and they fell asleep. They could not stay awake with him, so Jesus came out and woke them up and asked them again to stay awake and pray. But Jesus came back and found them asleep again. He could have gotten angry; he could have yelled and screamed at them and said, "Why can't you stay awake, you bums?" But Jesus never did that. In fact, every time Jesus was let down by his people and could have gotten angry at them, he never did! He always loved his disciples—and he always loves us, even in our weakness!

Because God loves us in our weakness, we can know that even now—when we sin because we get angry, when we are disappointed with how life is going, even when we are disappointed with God for not giving us what we want—Jesus's love for us never changes. He loves you so much that even when we disobey him, and he disciplines us, he does it out of love, not anger.

And on top of all this good stuff, Jesus keeps a treasure for us. This is so important for us to understand. Jesus does not keep anything back from us because he is disappointed with us. Instead he gives us everything we need.

HOW WE LIVE WITH LOVE

When we think we don't have what we need, the truth is that God promises to provide us with what we need. This changes us, and it changes how we treat each other. We are able to deal with disappointment because our God is a giving God. He is the God who knows what we need and provides for us. In fact, that is one of the names that the Bible uses to describe God: Jehovah-Jireh (Genesis 22:14). God's provision helps us to be content with what we have and to not always struggle for more.

In the middle of our disappointment over the way our lives are going, our God, Jehovah-Jireh, continues to provide. The fact that our God provides should give us joy! Joy that God loves us so much that he has given us everything we need and will give us more than we can ever ask for. This moves us to live patiently with the people who have disappointed us. But it does even more than that: it allows us to love those people and not hate them.

Talk 9
Strength

THEME: God gives men strength to serve and love others, not to control or intimidate them.

GETTING TO JESUS: Jesus was not only physically strong but also had access to unimaginable strength, yet he set that strength aside to serve us.

SUGGESTED ACTIVITY: Decide with your son on a needy person or family that you can help. If there is an older person at your church, go and do work that he or she needs around the house. Or perhaps you know a single dad or mom who would like some help with his or her kids?

How often have you tried to flex your muscles? (Why don't we have a flexing contest right now?) We have been given strength by God, and we can use that strength either to serve others or to get others to do what we want.

Have you ever tried to win a contest that has to do with strength? I coach baseball and this sort of thing happens all the time. The boys try to out-pushup each other, outrun each other, outhit each other, and on and on.

But we need to think about *why* God gave us our strength. We need to understand that our strength doesn't just have to do with our physical ability; it also has to do with our emotions and our convictions. Strength looks like a lot of different things in different people.

BOTH: When did you or someone you know have to show strength either physically, emotionally, or with their convictions? Talk about it.

WE WERE CREATED FOR THIS

Every man was created with strength—created to be strong. Adam was given the command to guard the garden of Eden; he was given the task of naming the animals and providing for Eve. It's not as if Eve didn't have muscles, emotions, or convictions; it is that God gave these tasks to Adam.

Adam was not created to use his strength to dominate others, but to carry out his role with love and compassion—and so are we. As Adam lived in love and service and as he carried out his role with strength, he was acting as God acts. As men, we are created to use our strength. Every time we do that in love for others, we are showing that man was created in the image of God.

Why? Because God uses his strength to guard, name, and provide.

Read Psalm 46:1–3: "God is our refuge and strength, a very present help in trouble. Therefore we will not fear though the earth gives way, though the mountains be moved into the heart of the sea, though its waters roar and foam, though the mountains tremble at its swelling."

Read Psalm 73:23–26: "Nevertheless, I am continually with you; you hold my right hand. You guide me with your counsel, and afterward you will receive me to glory. Whom have I in heaven but you? And there is nothing on earth that I desire besides you. My flesh and my heart may fail, but God is the strength of my heart and my portion forever."

DADS: How do you use your strength to imitate your heavenly Father?

SONS: Who do you know who uses his or her strength in love?

SIN HAS BROKEN US ALL

SONS: Have you ever known a bully? How did that bully use his or her strength?

This is how it happens: so often, men have used their strength to oppress people and not to protect. They have used their strength to build themselves up and tear other people down. This is a sad result of sin—what was given to men as a gift to help us live in the image of God has been twisted and used to abuse other people.

When we use our strength to bully other people or when we fail to stand up for those who are being bullied, we are showing how sin has broken all of us.

> **DADS:** When have you seen someone fail to use his or her strength to protect others? When have you failed to protect someone who was being bullied?

So often we fail to sacrifice ourselves and use our strength to protect others. These are all symptoms of sin's effects in our lives. One of Israel's kings, Rehoboam, showed how this happens. The people came to him, and asked him not to oppress them as his father did. This is what Rehoboam and his friends said:

Read 1 Kings 12:10, 14: "My little finger is thicker than my father's thighs. . . . My father made your yoke heavy, but I will add to your yoke. My father disciplined you with whips, but I will discipline you with scorpions."

Rehoboam used his power as king to intimidate the people of Israel. He used his strength to threaten to make other people miserable by forcing them to work more than they should. He used his position as king to bring glory to himself instead of bringing glory to God. When he should have guarded and protected the people who he was king over, he thought it more useful to hurt them. This would be like your teacher purposefully making your life miserable by giving you so much homework that you could never finish it—all just to prove that he was stronger than you.

JESUS DIED TO MAKE IT BETTER

Jesus was the strongest person ever to walk the planet. I don't mean that he had the biggest muscles, but that he had access to power that no other person did. When Jesus was about to be arrested, one of the disciples pulled out a sword and tried to kill someone to protect Jesus. Instead of letting him kill this man, Jesus healed the man. And then, he said something really important:

Read Matthew 26:52–54: "Put your sword back into its place. For all who take the sword will perish by the sword. Do you think that I cannot appeal to my Father, and he will at once send me more than twelve legions of angels? But how then should the Scriptures be fulfilled, that it must be so?"

Jesus had all the power of the universe at his fingertips, and yet he chose to use that power to die and fulfill the Scriptures so that we could be saved. He used his power to defeat Satan, sin, and death itself for us.

Jesus didn't need to use his power to bully people into following him. He used his power to love his enemies and to give them eternal life. And now, even when we fail to use our strength to serve others, we know that Jesus's perfect record of always serving is ours too.

HOW WE LIVE WITH LOVE

As followers of Jesus, we have this huge privilege of following after him. We don't have to bully others; instead, we can stand up for the people who are being bullied. When we see a victim of abuse or mistreatment, we can help him or her. When we see someone taken advantage of because they are not as strong as another person or have a disability, we can stand up for him or her. We can get a teacher, or we can protect that person ourselves; we can restrain the bully, or we can tell the bully to stop.

That is not all, though. When we see someone in need, we can use our strength to serve him or her. You can use the strength that God has given you to show his love to those around you. You can show God's strength to the sick and needy by bringing them food, changing a lightbulb, or mowing the lawn. These simple acts of love are pictures of God's strength at work in you.

BOTH: Think of some ways and/or some people you can serve in your church or in the local community.

Talk 10
Money

THEME: Money is a good thing, and God gives it to us so that we can learn to be generous—but it can begin to rule our lives.

GETTING TO JESUS: Jesus generously shares all his wealth with us, so that we can be rich in him.

SUGGESTED ACTIVITY: Think of ways you can use your money to serve the poor, underemployed, and/or homeless. Maybe you can talk to a deacon or elder at your church about what you could do specifically.

Money is pretty cool. We can do fun things with money, can't we? You can buy a new fishing rod, baseball bat, or video game with it, and all those things are a bunch of fun. A lot of the time, though, people—people who want to follow God—think there is something wrong with having money. In fact, they may even tell you that the Bible says money is the root of all evil. But money is not evil, riches are not evil—that's not actually what the Bible says (we'll get to that a little later). How we *use* that money can be sinful, though. You see, buddy, we all take the good things that God gives us and use them to serve ourselves. And when we do that, we make the good thing more important than God.

WE WERE CREATED FOR THIS

The Bible has a lot to say about money, because God knows that we want things that are valuable. If someone walked up to you right now and offered you one million dollars, would you take it? Of course, you would. Why? Because of our desire for things, for power, and to look better in front of others.

In the beginning, God told Adam that everything in the garden was his.

Read Genesis 1:29: "Behold, I have given you every plant yielding seed that is on the face of all the earth, and every tree with seed in its fruit. You shall have them for food."

You see, God created us so that everything on the planet would be ours and so that we would enjoy it all. We were created to enjoy God's good gifts to us—and money is one of those good gifts.

DADS: What are some of the good things that God has given you that you enjoy?

SONS: What is the one thing that God has given you that you are most thankful for?

SIN HAS BROKEN US ALL

Sin has messed up the way that we use and pursue money. Now, instead of being a good thing used to serve others and enjoy God with, money often tears us apart. It makes us jealous, angry, sad, and selfish. We want to keep our money in order to make ourselves happy.

Adam and Eve had everything in the garden, and Satan tempted them with something else. Satan offered them something they thought they didn't have, and they took it. Because they selfishly took what they wanted, sin entered the world and changed the way we think about and use God's good gifts. We often don't use them to serve others, but only to serve ourselves.

When Jesus was about to die, one of his friends sold him for thirty pieces of silver. Think about that: Jesus's friend sold him—betrayed him for money. He sold Jesus to the authorities so that they could kill him.

Read Matthew 26:14–16: "Then one of the twelve, whose name was Judas Iscariot, went to the chief priests and said, 'What will you give me if I deliver him over to you?' And they paid him thirty pieces of silver. And from that moment he sought an opportunity to betray him."

BOTH: Talk about what it would be like to have one of your best friends betray you.

Sin will make people do anything for money. People have sold other people over time—sold them into slavery and death. That is absolutely wrong, and God hates it, but here is the beautiful thing: Jesus allowed himself to be sold and killed so that we would no longer be a slave to our stuff and our money.

JESUS DIED TO MAKE IT BETTER

When Jesus was betrayed and killed, it wasn't just because Judas took money and sold Jesus. We all participate in Jesus's death because all of us are selfish and are willing to use our money, stuff, and other people to make us happy. But Jesus didn't just die to make things better; he also lived so that when God looks at us, he doesn't see our sin of selfishness. Instead, he sees Jesus's generosity.

Read 2 Corinthians 8:9: "For you know the grace of our Lord Jesus Christ, that though he was rich, yet for your sake he became poor, so that you by his poverty might become rich."

Even though Jesus had everything, he didn't keep it for himself. He didn't use his riches to take advantage of us; he didn't sell us—he gave up himself for us. He gave up his riches so that we would be rich—not with money but through a relationship with God himself. The really amazing thing is he did this when we were enemies.

> **DADS**: What would it be like to give up everything you own, so that your enemies would become rich?
>
> **SONS**: What about you? Would you ever give up all your toys or games to the school bully—right after he bullied you?

That is what makes Jesus so amazing! Jesus loves us so much that he didn't hesitate to give up everything and die for us.

LIVING WITH LOVE

The truth of what Jesus did for us should make us very generous with our money. Money is a good thing, a gift from God that we get to use to serve other people, especially people who are suffering.

God gave us church deacons, who have the job of using money to serve the poor (Acts 6:1–7). But it is not just deacons who get to help; we can help the poor as well. This is the awesome thing about Jesus: he gives us everything we need and then he gives us the Holy Spirit so that we can fight against the love of money. Do you remember the verse at the beginning of our talk that people get wrong? What those verses actually say is this:

Read 1 Timothy 6:6–10:

> But godliness with contentment is great gain, for we brought nothing into the world, and we cannot take anything out of the world. But if we have food and clothing, with these we will be content. But those who desire to be rich fall into temptation, into a snare, into many senseless and harmful desires that plunge people into ruin and destruction. For the love of money is a root of all kinds of evils.

Jesus has made us into new people—people who do not serve their money, but instead use their money to serve other people. This is so cool. That does not mean that we cannot ever use our money to buy things we like, but it does mean that what we like isn't what we live for. We don't live to own a Lego set; we don't get life from our video games or our fishing gear. Our bike didn't serve us and die. And when we use our money to serve ourselves, we can ask Jesus to forgive us—and he will. That is a God who is much better than our money.

> **BOTH:** Based on your conversation at the beginning of this lesson, make a specific plan for practicing generosity using the ideas you discussed together.

Talk 11
Girls

THEME: Girls are cool, fun, good friends, and they deserve our respect, care, and love.

GETTING TO JESUS: Jesus respected and loved women. He gave them a dignified place, even as the society around them demeaned them. We reflect Jesus when we also love and respect women.

SUGGESTED ACTIVITY: Spend some time together, first talking through the chapter, and then talk to a woman who can help you and your son understand what it is like to be a girl in today's society.

Girls are pretty cool. They can be very nice, creative, athletic, smart, and just plain interesting. Because they are different from guys, sometimes they do things we guys don't understand. Sometimes we think they are weak or dumb, but that's a wrong way to think about someone who sees things differently from us. God is so great that he knew guys and girls need each other. He knew that women would display his glory in a way that us guys can't.

But sometimes we don't know how to relate to women (or girls). They can seem strange and that can make us nervous. They can be stronger or smarter than us and that can feel threatening. Some guys see girls and think only about how they can use them to make themselves feel good. This is not okay. Women are made in the image of God and deserve the love and respect that every child of God deserves.

WE WERE CREATED FOR THIS

When God made so many of the creatures in the garden of Eden, he made them in pairs—and God said they were good. But when God created Adam, he saw that he was alone, and that it was not good. So God created Eve, and Adam said, "This at last is bone of my bones and flesh of my flesh" (Genesis 2:23). Together Adam and Eve were the first family, and soon they had children, just as your mom and I had you. God made Adam and Eve different, but they were alike in that they both were made in God's image. That hasn't changed. Both boys and girls, although different, are made in God's image and have dignity and value.

> **SONS:** What girl are you good friends with? What makes you friends? What do you like about her?

Women are important to God. They were created in the image of God, just like we were. Women deserve respect, care, and encouragement because God has made them in his image. They were not created to be blamed, used, or made fun of.

SIN HAS BROKEN US ALL

We have already talked about Adam and Eve and how they decided to go their own way and not believe in God's love for them. After Eve took the fruit, ate it, and gave it to Adam, all their troubles began—including conflict between each other (Genesis 3:16). It was not only Eve's fault for eating the fruit, as some men say. Adam failed to guard Eve, to respect her by protecting her and guarding the garden, and Satan deceived her. What was once a beautiful relationship, where Adam and Eve could live together and not be ashamed, was spoiled.

Now the relationship between men and women is all too often messed up by sin. Sadly, men often use women for their own pleasure. Men abuse women, using either physical violence or saying mean things to them, to make women feel bad and do what they want.

This is not what God wanted. God doesn't want relationships to operate this way. When men use, abuse, or intimidate women, they show the curse of sin in this world. They give in to sin's powerful effect on their lives. Instead of being mean to the girls in your life or even just staying away from them, God wants us to be kind to them and work at being friends.

SONS: How do you struggle to be friends with girls? What girls are you friends with? How did you become friends?

DADS: How have you seen men struggle to respect women?

JESUS DIED TO MAKE IT BETTER

Throughout his whole life, Jesus respected women. He valued them and showed how valuable they were. Women were never a burden to him; they were never weird or a hassle. Remember, Jesus lived in a society where women were looked at like they were nothing. People didn't respect women; they treated women like they were possessions.

Jesus loved and befriended women, even those women who might not be welcome in our churches. He never used them for his own pleasure; instead, when he was with women who could not protect themselves, he protected them and became their friend. Jesus redeemed a woman who had a terrible reputation (Luke 7:36–50) . At a time when women were not even trusted to tell the truth, Jesus appeared to Mary, a woman, and told her to tell everyone about his resurrection (John 20:11–18).

You see, Jesus valued women—and still does. Women were important to the spread of Christianity. Women paid for the apostles' ministry and prayed for the advancement of the gospel. Priscilla helped support and train one of the most influential preachers in the Bible, Apollos (Acts 18:18–28). Romans 16:1–16 is full of descriptions of women who were important members of the church—serving, sacrificing their own safety, supporting, and working hard for the Lord.

Jesus values women. He sees them as his sisters. He also died for men who don't value women. He died to pay the penalty for everyone who asks for forgiveness. And with his death, the reconciling work of God works inside of us to make us people who respect and love women too.

LIVING WITH LOVE

Because Jesus has died to forgive us of our sins, we can show his love and honor toward the women in our lives. As men, we can respect women and encourage them to be all that God has created them to be. We don't have to tear women down so that we can feel better about ourselves. Instead, we can live a life of friendship and service with women.

Read 1 Timothy 5:1–2: "Do not rebuke an older man but encourage him as you would a father . . . older women as mothers, younger women as sisters, in all purity."

God wants you to treat older women with the same respect and care that you have for your mom. God wants you to treat girls like you would your sister—be friends and stick up for them if someone is picking on them. Listen to what they have to say and make sure you value their opinions.

Read Acts 18:26: "He [Apollos] began to speak boldly in the synagogue, but when Priscilla and Aquila heard him, they took him aside and explained to him the way of God more accurately."

Son, the way you live with love when it comes to women is to see them as people made in the image of God, who are to be served and loved. We don't look at them as objects to use, but see them for who they are—our mothers and sisters in the family of God, worthy of respect, honor, and love. We can become friends with them, learn to like what they like, and do what they do—even when it's not always what *we* would enjoy doing. We can value their opinions and cherish their thoughts. We also live with love by protecting women who we see being hurt by men. We can stick up for them when they are bullied or made fun of, and encourage them when they're discouraged or disappointed.

This is how we live with love—we love women like Jesus loved them.

Talk 12
Sex

THEME: God created sex, and he made it good. We need to tell the Bible's good story of God's plan for sex.

> **Note:** It would be good to start talking to your son about sex and sexuality whenever he begins to ask questions and definitely at the first sign that he is interested in the development of his body and sexuality. This may be at six or at eight. There is no special formula for when to have "the sex talk." The point is you may need to go slow with this talk. Be open and allow him to ask questions. For a more in-depth treatment on this subject I coauthored a book titled *Mom, Dad . . . What's Sex?*. You may want to look through that book as well as *God Made All of Me*[1] by Justin and Lindsey Holcomb for the younger crowd.

GETTING TO JESUS: Jesus makes everything whole, including our sexuality.

---

1. Jessica Thompson and Joel Fitzpatrick, *Mom, Dad . . . What's Sex?* (Eugene, OR: Harvest House, 2018). *God Made All of Me* (Greensboro, NC: New Growth Press, 2015).

SUGGESTED ACTIVITY: This is more of a private conversation and probably calls for sitting in the backyard.

Buddy, today's talk may get a little bit awkward, and we may have to talk about some things that seem strange to you.

So first, I want to tell you that I love you. If you have any questions that you want to ask me, please do. Don't wait; I won't be bothered by them.

Second, you need to know that, as Christians, we learn about sex from what God says. A lot of people think that Christians are narrow-minded because the way God talks about sex is different from what the world around us says. Something to keep in mind is that God's way brings blessing and protection for your body and heart. Because God is our loving and wise creator and because he designed sex, he is the expert we listen to. When we don't listen to God and follow his good plans, we only hurt ourselves and others. This has been true about everything we've discussed so far, and it's just as true about sex.

You need to hear this from me, son: God loves you, and you need to be careful with sex. But you also need to know that God forgives people who sin sexually. It's never okay to sin, but when we do sin and ask God for forgiveness, he still loves us and forgives us.

SONS: Are you okay with us talking about sex?

WE WERE CREATED FOR THIS

Read Genesis 2:25: "And the man and his wife were both naked and were not ashamed."

Read Genesis 1:28: "And God blessed them. And God said to them, 'Be fruitful and multiply and fill the earth and subdue it, and have dominion . . . over every living thing that moves on the earth.'"

When God created Adam and Eve, he put them together in the garden. And here is something kind of awkward: the Bible says that they were naked but had no shame. They weren't embarrassed; they were happy. It wasn't wrong. God gave Eve to Adam and Adam to Eve, and he told them to have babies and that was good. God said that his creation was "very good" once Adam and Eve were together in the garden (Genesis 1:31).

Buddy, God created our bodies with nerves and chemicals that make us want to have sex, and that make it feel good. This is one of the reasons God created sex: so that we would get joy from it. (The book of the Song of Solomon talks a lot about the pleasure of sex. Also, see Proverbs 5:15–19.) Your body is going through changes that are perfectly normal and natural. In fact, it was created by God to function the way it does.

Sometimes it feels unnatural for our body to act the way it does. But God has created your body and that is not bad. Sex was made so that when a man and a woman marry they can express their love for each other in a special way just for them. God made sex for one man and one woman to enjoy with each other only after they married and promised to love only each other.

SONS: Do you understand? Do you have any questions?

SIN HAS BROKEN US ALL

But when sin came into the world, people took God's good gift and started to use it to serve themselves. The Bible talks about this all over the place. One of the first bad guys in the Bible took advantage of women and had multiple wives (Genesis 4:23–24). Even King David, who was a man after God's own heart, took advantage of his power as a king to take advantage of a woman (2 Samuel 11).

This is the problem that we have seen so many times—sin breaks the good things that God has given us to enjoy him. The Bible warns us about the danger of sexual sin. It brings so much pain, and God wants to keep us and the women we love from that pain.

Read Proverbs 6:32: "He who commits adultery lacks sense; he who does it destroys himself."

Read Proverbs 7:24–27: "And now, O sons, listen to me, and be attentive to the words of my mouth. Let not your heart turn aside to her ways; do not stray into her paths, for many a victim has she laid low, and all her slain are a mighty throng. Her house is the way to Sheol, going down to the chambers of death."

What God meant to be a special gift between just one man and one woman who are married together has been used to do all kinds of hurtful and mean things.

These things hurt the people who do them and they hurt others too. It's sad that people use God's good gift to hurt others. Have you ever seen that happen or heard about it? (This would be a good time to hear from your son about the conversations he and his friends are having and what things he has seen).

Did you know that Jesus says that if we even lust after a woman in our hearts we have sinned sexually? Because we are all sinful beings, we have to be on our guard against all kinds of sexual sin.

Buddy, if anyone tries to touch you where you're not comfortable being touched, you need to know that it is not your fault. Please tell me or someone you trust right away if that happens—no matter what the person who touched you might say. I will always love you and will not be ashamed of you. You will not get in trouble, you will not be hated; we will continue to love you.

People also use sex in the wrong way by looking at pictures and videos of people having sex. This is called pornography. God gave us sex to be enjoyed between one man and one woman for their whole life—not as something to watch other people do. This is another way that sin has messed up our world. If someone shows you pictures or videos like that, tell them that you don't want to see them. And then let me or your mom know, and we can talk together about what happened.

> **SONS:** Do you have any questions so far? Again, it's okay to ask.

JESUS DIED TO MAKE IT BETTER

Praise God that Jesus didn't leave us with all this pain and brokenness. He didn't stay away from us, but he came to save people who are sinners. Buddy, did you know that there were a lot of people who sinned sexually, but were redeemed and used by God in the Bible—even some of Jesus's ancestors? Jesus isn't ashamed of sexually broken people. In fact, Jesus loves to save sinners.

The apostle Paul talked about the relationship between Jesus and the church (Ephesians 5:22–33). He even went so far to say that it's like a marriage. Paul said that Jesus is the husband and the church is his bride. That means that Jesus wants us to think of the closeness that is experienced in marriage—yes, even in sex—and tells us that it's kind of like his love for us. Jesus gives himself up to meet our needs. He loves us purely, and he wants his church to experience intimacy with him. When Jesus returns, he will bring all Christians into a marriage feast (Revelation 19:6–9), where we will celebrate the kind of love, joy, reunion, and intimacy that married couples experience—and so much more. And the best part of this is that we don't deserve to be brought into this sort of relationship with him. We can't earn his love. We can't make Jesus feel any more love or intimacy toward us than he already does. Jesus loves us even though we are sinners, and he makes us his perfect spotless bride.

Jesus loves sinners, saves sinners, redeems sinners and then uses them in his kingdom. This is so amazing. He doesn't just use perfect people. In fact, Jesus uses people who sin pretty badly. For example, Rahab the prostitute is one of his ancestors. Jesus also let a "sinful woman" (many scholars say she was a prosti-tute) wash, kiss, and anoint his feet, and then told her that her sins were forgiven (Luke 7:36–50). King David was called a man after God's own heart, even though he sinned by sleeping with another man's wife and then had her husband killed. God is not ashamed to use sinful people who turn to him and repent of their sins. He isn't afraid to call sinful people his bride.

> **SONS:** Do you have any questions?

LIVING WITH LOVE

All of this means that what God tells us about how sex is supposed to go is also right and good. When God says that sex is only for marriage, we should see that as a good blessing. It is kind of like when I tell you the best way to use a tool—I want what is best for you, and I don't want you to be hurt. I want you to experi-ence blessing.

It's the same with God. And this is how we live with love for the people around us. When you know some-one has been touched inappropriately, you tell me. When you're tempted to look at inappropriate pictures or videos, you stop and ask God for forgiveness. You can tell me about that too, and we can pray together. We look for ways to help people who are being taken advantage of sexually.

It also means that we fight against the tempta-tion to give in to sexual desire. Instead, we fall in love with Jesus and pursue satisfaction in him. If we do sin, though, we know that Jesus will forgive our sin and cleanse us from all unrighteousness.

Talk 13
Defending Others

THEME: As followers of Christ, we are called to defend anyone who is weak. God tells his people to defend the poor, widows, fatherless, immigrants, and those who are being oppressed. In this talk we will cover issues like racism, charity, sticking up for others, and self-sacrifice.

GETTING TO JESUS: Jesus came to us when we were dead, and now he defends us from Satan's accusations.

SUGGESTED ACTIVITY: Go on a walk, buy a newspaper, and look through it with your son. Pick out stories that talk about those who are weak and need defending. Then talk about who in your lives are being put down, discriminated against, wrongly accused, or bullied, and what you can do to help put a stop to it.

S on, we live in a pretty amazing country. We are free to talk about stuff that people around the world wish they could talk about. We can talk about politics. We can say our government is wrong. We can read our Bibles in public. We are free to worship God without fear of the government. But our country wasn't always free for all people, and there are still parts of our society where humans are looked down on, not trusted, and even treated differently because they have a different skin color or are poor, widows, fatherless, or homeless.

It can be hard to be friends with people who are not like us, because we don't want to be challenged. It is hard to defend your friends because it can be scary, especially if we have to defend them from someone attacking them. It is even harder to defend people who are different than us. That takes something special working in and on us—a new spirit, a new heart.

> **SONS:** Why is it hard to love people who are not like us?

WE WERE CREATED FOR THIS

When God made Adam and Eve, he made two people—not one person and not two people with the same personality. Then they had children, who had more children, who moved to different parts of the world, who developed different skin colors. All these people who are different are made in the image of God.

The apostle Paul also gave us a great illustration of this when he described the church as one body, made of many different parts.

Read 1 Corinthians 12:14–20:

> For the body does not consist of one member but of many. If the foot should say, "Because I am not a hand, I do not belong to the body," that would not make it any less a part of the body. And if the ear should say, "Because I am not an eye, I do not belong to the body," that would not make it any less a part of the body. If the whole body were an eye, where would be the sense of hearing? If the whole body were an ear, where would be the sense of smell? But as it is, God arranged the members in the body, each one of them, as he chose. If all were a single member, where would the body be? As it is, there are many parts, yet one body.

We need people who are different from us, and God loves people who are different. In fact, God created us to be different, but still one body in Christ.

BOTH: How can different types of people help each other do things they're usually not good at?

But sometimes, when people are really different from us or those around us, they get picked on. Adam was told to guard (protect) the garden and that included his wife, Eve—not just because he had bigger muscles, but because when we protect people we are acting the way God acts. God loves people who are different. He cares for orphans, provides for widows, and rescues people who are oppressed. God loves the homeless and provides them with what they need.

Read Psalm 68:5: "Father of the fatherless and protector of widows is God in his holy habitation."

Read Deuteronomy 10:18: "He executes justice for the fatherless and the widow, and loves the sojourner, giving him food and clothing."

SIN HAS BROKEN US ALL

But the sad reality is that since sin entered the world, we no longer look at different people and think about protecting them. Sadly, we think about ignoring, making fun of, or even attacking them. Now, when we run into people who look or act different than us, we often automatically don't like them. We may even be afraid of them. We see people and only notice what's different about them. We forget about the thing that is similar: We are all made in the image of God.

This is a sad and hard truth. It is one of the reasons why it can be so hard to go to a new school or church, or to play on a new sports team. We're afraid we won't fit in and that people will pick on us.

> **DADS**: What sort of things do you notice about other people who are different from you?
>
> **SONS**: When have you been picked on for being different? How did it make you feel?

When someone gets picked on because he or she is different, we know we should defend that person—but it is so hard. We're afraid that we too will get picked on, or even hurt. That fear can stop us from standing up for that person, even when we know we should. Sin has even broken our ability to defend others.

JESUS DIED TO MAKE IT BETTER

What is so great about Jesus is that he never once shied away from defending people. In fact, Jesus became a man not only to defend us, but to defeat our enemies. When we were enemies of God—when we were so very different from God—he became a man. He became our friend.

Read John 15:15: "No longer do I call you servants . . . but I have called you friends."

Jesus did this for us so that we would know what it is like to have a protector, a defender, for our friend. But he didn't do it because we are good or because we are worth defending. He did it because he knew that without him, we would be defenseless.

The amazing thing is that Jesus didn't just defend us by dying for us—he is still defending us. Did you know that Satan is not the devil's only name? He is also known as the accuser of Christians (Revelation 12:10). Every time you or I sin, Satan brings it up to God; he tells God of all the wrong things that we have done. But Jesus defends us to the Father. He constantly prays for us and constantly reminds the Father that our sins are forgiven because of his work on the cross.

This is what Jesus does for us. He defends us in so many ways. He always has, and always will, defend us.

Read Romans 8:38–39: "For I am sure that neither death nor life, nor angels nor rulers, not things present nor things to come, nor powers, nor height nor depth, nor anything else in all creation, will be able to separate us from the love of God in Christ Jesus our Lord."

BOTH: How does it make you feel that God's love defends us and that it can never go away?

LIVING WITH LOVE

The truth is that defending others is hard. It is scary. We need someone to defend us, so that when we step out and defend others we can trust that God is with us. That may not stop us from getting punched or made fun of—after all, Jesus promised that we would have trouble when we follow and obey him (John 16:33)—but it does mean that God will protect us.

God gives us the strength and courage to stand up for people who are being bullied. Maybe it is someone whose skin color is different than most people in your town who needs you to stand up for him or her. You may get beat up for it, made fun of, or called nasty names, but this is exactly what we are called to do in Jesus's name. Maybe it is someone who has a learning disability who is being picked on who needs you to stand up for him or her. When you do this, you are acting like Jesus. You are being who Jesus has made you to be; you are doing what Jesus wants you to do. Maybe when you see an entire group of people who is in power oppressing a group of people without power (for example, a community of refugees or the homeless), you can say or do something to help these powerless people.

This could also happen in school. If you see a person with disabilities being bullied by the popular kids, pray that God would give you the strength and courage to defend that person. You could go and defend the person being bullied, or you could go and get a teacher, or you could stand between the person being bullied and the bully.

Or maybe there are people in your neighborhood who don't fit in because they look different, have different accents, or eat different foods. This is an amazing opportunity to become their friend.

Jesus has broken down all the things that make us different from each other. When we become Christians, all the things that might have separated us from each other are done away with.

Read Galatians 3:27–28: "For as many of you as were baptized into Christ have put on Christ. There is neither Jew nor Greek, there is neither slave nor free, there is no male and female, for you are all one in Christ Jesus."

BOTH: What would life be like if you didn't focus on the things that make you different, but on the things that make you similar? Who can you befriend or help defend right now who's different from you? How?

Talk 14
Heaven

THEME: God has a home prepared for us when we die, and he is keeping that home ready for the day when he returns for us.

GETTING TO JESUS: Jesus won heaven for us, so that we can live with him for eternity.

SUGGESTED ACTIVITY: It would be ideal if you can have this talk after a big party, such as a birthday or wedding. This will take some forethought, but it is such a great opportunity to demonstrate the sense of joy and celebration we are talking about.

> **BOTH:** What do you think heaven is going to be like?

Death can be a very scary thing. No one has died recently and then come back and told us what heaven was like. When I was growing up, I was always afraid that heaven was going to be a boring place—like going to church all the time. I didn't want anything to do with that. But what the Bible says about heaven is so much different. Heaven is this amazing place where we are with God and experience joy all the time.

Read John 14:2–3: "In my Father's house are many rooms. If it were not so, would I have told you that I go to prepare a place for you? And if I go to prepare a place for you, I will come again and will take you to myself, that where I am you may be also."

Read Revelation 7:15–17: "Therefore they are before the throne of God, and serve him day and night in his temple; and he who sits on the throne will shelter them with his presence. They shall hunger no more, neither thirst anymore; the sun shall not strike them, nor any scorching heat. For the Lamb in the midst of the throne will be their shepherd, and he will guide them to springs of living water, and God will wipe away every tear from their eyes."

This is something that is really hard to understand: joy, fulfillment, happiness, and friendship all the time. Right now, that may seem like a little bit much, but in heaven we will never get sick of it.

WE WERE CREATED FOR THIS

Heaven is going to be so cool. When they were created, Adam and Eve experienced what heaven was like, but only in part. Even in the garden of Eden, they did not experience this sort of joy. Take a second and imagine that: when everything was right in the world—and nothing was broken, sad, and stained by sin—even that time cannot compare with heaven.

Read Revelation 21:1–3:

> Then I saw a new heaven and a new earth, for the first heaven and the first earth had passed away, and the sea was no more. And I saw the holy city, new Jerusalem, coming down out of heaven from God, prepared as a bride adorned for her husband. And I heard a loud voice from the throne saying, "Behold, the dwelling place of God is with man. He will dwell with them, and they will be his people, and God himself will be with them as their God."

Read 1 Corinthians 15:42–44: "So is it with the resurrection of the dead. What is sown is perishable; what is raised is imperishable. It is sown in dishonor; it is raised in glory. It is sown in weakness; it is raised in power. It is sown a natural body; it is raised a spiritual body. If there is a natural body, there is also a spiritual body."

The new earth will be where we live for eternity. Our bodies will be remade perfectly; there will be no suffering and no crying for all of eternity. Imagine that: the new earth is going to have the best of everything, and we will get to enjoy it forever. In the new earth, we will get to enjoy all the best things of life forever because we will be with God.

If Adam and Eve had obeyed, this would already have been ours; we would have never had to have lived in a broken, sin-cursed world. They would have passed the test and been given all these blessings, and we would have been able to live such different lives.

SONS: What are ten things you would like to do in heaven?

DADS: Who would you want to see in heaven?

SIN HAS BROKEN US ALL

What should have been ours—what could have been ours if Adam and Eve had obeyed—was lost. Now, what we live with is the opposite of what it should be. Our bodies get hurt; we cry when things don't go our way. We get angry at each other when the other person doesn't do what we want them to do. Our stuff breaks. Sometimes it even gets stolen. Instead of work being fun and enjoyable like it was in the garden, it is difficult.

BOTH: Can you remember a time when you lost something valuable to you?

This is what happened when sin entered the world: everything that was good was messed up. Even the trees, grass, wind, and rain have suffered. Now after the fall, even good things like peanuts can kill people. Bees sting, ants bite, and dogs die. Even the best things in life die; they come to an end. Son, someday even I am going to die. This is the hard thing about this world.

It may be when I am ninety or it may be before that. Because of sin, death entered the world.

JESUS DIED TO MAKE IT BETTER

In the middle of all this death, all this pain, there is only one person who is strong enough to make it better and it is not you or me—it's Jesus. Jesus died to undo all the wrongs that sin had brought into the world. What I love about Jesus is that he is God, and that he could have stayed in heaven and done what was easy. But he didn't. He saw the pain, he saw the suffering that sin had brought on the world, he saw the death, and he knew that the only way to beat sin was to die himself. And that is exactly what he did. He died to overcome sin's power.

Because Jesus did that there is hope—hope based in the reality that Jesus has given us a home, so that when we die we have a place with him. That place is being prepared for us; it is ours. When we believe in Jesus, he gives us a home in heaven, where everything that is wrong will be made right.

But the best part is that God loves us and wants to be with us for eternity. Our relationship is changed from being separated because of our sin to being part of God's family. And we get to live this way forever, always living in light of God the Father's blessing.

Read John 14:1–4 (NIV): "Do not let your hearts be troubled. You believe in God; believe also in me. My Father's house has many rooms; if that were not so, would I have told you that I am going there to prepare a place for you? And if I go and prepare a place for you, I will come back and take you to be with me that you also may be where I am. You know the way to the place where I am going."

This has been God's plan all along. Heaven was what he knew we needed, so that is what he planned for us. But it gets better. Jesus isn't just saving heaven for us—he is preparing something even better. He is making the new earth, where we will have new bodies and won't experience death, pain, or sorrow.

Read Revelation 21:4: "He will wipe away every tear from their eyes, and death shall be no more, neither shall there be mourning, nor crying, nor pain anymore, for the former things have passed away."

This is what Jesus is preparing for us. It will be amazing. When we think about what the new earth might be like, we might think of a home on a beach with perfect waves all the time or a forest with big hills and lots of mushrooms to pick. Whatever comes to your mind, God has something even better in mind for you.

BOTH: What do you think your home on the new earth will be like? Use your imagination. Encourage your son that no matter what he imagines, the new earth will be better.

LIVING WITH LOVE

When we live with this hope, we live with love—because we don't want to keep this hope to ourselves. Remember what Jesus said in John 14:2: "In my Father's house are many rooms." This means that there is more than enough space for everyone to come in.

This also gives us comfort when we are sad. When people we love who are Christians die, we can know that they are no longer suffering, that Jesus has welcomed them home, and that they are at rest in the presence of Jesus.

So we tell others about the hope that we have been given. We invite them to believe, so that they can have this hope as well. We show love for our neighbors by telling them about Jesus.

Conclusion

You did it! You made it to the end. Well done. I hope that this series of walks and talks with your son has helped strengthen your relationship together—and both of your relationships with God. I'm sure that some of these talks have been hard, but the benefits you will experience, having had them, will outweigh the discomforts.

It is my sincerest desire that this season of discussions is the start of a lifetime of life-shaping conversations between you and your son as he grows older.

You may be at the end of this book and may be walking around with low-level guilt for not having done these conversations perfectly. Don't worry, no one is able to have perfect conversations with their boys. The point is to make the effort to engage with them—to point them to Jesus. You won't be a perfect dad, and that's okay. Your son's desire for Christ is not based on that.

Our sons don't need our perfection. They need us to be faithful, humble witnesses of Christ's work in us. God calls you to be faithful and to point your son to Jesus. May God bless you, as you continue a lifetime of conversations with your son.

Appendix A
What Is the Gospel?

This seems like such a simple question to answer. We have all been taught that the gospel is that Jesus died for our sins. But the gospel is so much more than that. The gospel is not just about keeping us out of hell—although that alone is really cool. The gospel is about the life, death, and resurrection of Christ.

As you have been talking with your son, you have been explaining this whole gospel. You have been telling the good news of what Jesus has done for you, and the new relationship that results from Jesus's work on our behalf. Good news—that is what the word *gospel* means. It is good news meant to be told to the people around us. Let's walk through this.

What follows is a shortened description of the gospel, in three parts. There are books upon books written describing this topic. If you're looking for something more in depth, I would suggest reading *Because He Loves Me* by Elyse Fitzpatrick and *The Whole Christ* by Sinclair Ferguson.

THE LIFE OF JESUS

God made a promise (back then they called that a *covenant*) with Adam in the garden of Eden, and later with Israel as his people. He gave them the law, and told them that if they kept the law they would live. Adam and Israel failed—and so do we today. Because we can't keep the whole law (God calls this *sin*), we can't live with God forever in heaven. Since God is holy and perfect, we can't be with him unless we too are completely holy and perfect (the Bible calls this *righteousness*).

This is why the life of Jesus is so important. He obeyed all of the law, and now he gives us his righteousness so that when the Father looks at us he sees the righteousness of Christ (Romans 5; 8:1–4; Galatians 3:27). One easy illustration of this is in the game of baseball: if one team member hits a home run, everyone benefits by getting a run for the team. In much the same way, we get the benefits of Jesus's obedience.

THE DEATH OF JESUS

There was a penalty to be paid because of our sin—death. Either we pay that penalty or someone else pays it. Everyone who dies and isn't a believer in Jesus pays that penalty in hell, separated from God forever. But for believers in Christ, Jesus's death paid the penalty for us. He took away God's wrath, so that now there is nothing left but God's love for us (Mark 10:45; Romans 8:31–35; 1 John 2:2). Jesus's death cancels the debt that we owe for our sin.

THE RESURRECTION OF JESUS

The gospel doesn't just stop there, though. It includes Jesus's resurrection. The apostle Paul talked about how the resurrection confirms that Jesus succeeded in saving his people: "It will be counted to us who believe in him who raised from the dead Jesus our Lord, who was delivered up for our trespasses and raised for our justification" (Romans 4:24–25).

And here is even better news: just as Jesus was raised from the dead, you will be too. Paul said that if the resurrection isn't true then Christians should be pitied more than anyone else, because the resurrection is of utmost importance (1 Corinthians 15:19). But the resurrection is true. And now that Jesus is raised from the dead, he is praying for us (Romans 8:34).

This is why we need to tell our boys the full gospel. They need to know that it is only through faith that they are made right with God. They come to salvation through faith in Jesus.

So, what is faith? There are three parts: believing, receiving, and resting. We believe that the gospel is true (Romans 10:9–10). We receive it as true for us, seeing that we were dead in our trespasses and sins (Ephesians 2:1–3). Then we rest in Jesus's work for us. We see that there is nothing we can do to save ourselves (Ephesians 2:8–9). Jesus did it all—for us. And that is good news.

Sharing the gospel with your son is both incredibly simple and also very humbling. It is simple because it is just a matter of talking and living like you are a free person—a man who is free from the crushing effects of the law. It is as simple as talking about the gospel when your son sins, pointing him to Christ. It is as simple as seeing your son as a sinner in need of grace—just like you.

As dads, we cannot expect our sons to be any more perfect than we are. Therefore, we need to be patient in their failures, just as the Father is patient with us. We can show them the forgiveness of God by being quick to forgive them and restore them (Luke 15:11–32).

This is simple to say, and difficult to do. So, here are a few helpful hints.

First, talk about the goodness of the gospel. When you can, connect the gospel with what they are experiencing in a natural way. Here's an example: if your son gets mad at his sibling and yells or hits them, after you stop the violence, tell him the good news that Jesus had brothers and sisters too. No doubt they took his stuff sometimes, but he never got sinfully angry with them. Tell your son that when we have faith in Jesus, God sees us as if we had never gotten angry, because we are covered with Christ's righteousness (Isaiah 61:10; 2 Corinthians 5:21). When we put our faith in Jesus, we are given a new heart in exchange for our old, dead one (2 Corinthians 5:17; Hebrews 8:10). We are no longer controlled by the flesh but by the Spirit (Romans 8:9).

Second, remind them that God loves and forgives them. Point out where you already see God at work in them. And here is the kicker: when we sin against our sons, we ask for their forgiveness and remind them that we need the gospel just as much as they do. We tell them that the Holy Spirit lives in both of us and has set us free from sin (2 Corinthians 3:17).

Third, we pray for them. We pray that God would grip their hearts with the truths of the gospel.

Finally, involve them in a church where they hear the gospel every week and where they can participate in the sacraments (Communion and baptism). Encourage them that God speaks to them through the teaching of his Word. Remind them that baptism signifies the reality that God is making a covenant with them. And tell them that just as surely as they see and taste the bread and wine, Jesus was sacrificed for them and is committed to them forever.

See, dads, it is simple but also hard. Sharing the gospel with your sons requires that you be plugged in to their lives—and the gospel—as you live with them. It means that you are paying attention to the work of Christ in your home. You can do this.

Appendix C
How Do I Lead Family Worship?

Family worship is a lost art in American Christianity. It may even sound mysterious because it is so foreign to us. It may also feel boring and legalistic. But it doesn't have to be boring, and it isn't legalistic. It is simply leading your family to Christ through the ordinary means of the Word and prayer. It is the simple practice of reading the Bible today—maybe explaining the passage, maybe asking questions—and then praying.

This sounds like a daunting task, because for the majority of us (myself included), our wives are more spiritually aware than we are. But when a man leads his family to church and in worship, his family understands that God is a priority in his life, and they will be very likely to follow him in it.

Now to the mechanics of it. There are two core elements: the Word and prayer. The rest is up to you.

Open your time together with prayer. Your family may like to sing; if so, sing a song you sing at church. If not, make a joyful noise—try a song anyway, and laugh. Singing is so helpful for remembering the truths of God. If you need help with songs, Seeds Family Worship (a band) sets Scripture to good music geared toward family worship.

Then, open your Bible. Starting with one of the Gospels is a great place. Read a portion of Scripture, and ask the kids simple questions about the story line. Then ask them about how they see Jesus in the passage—as the person who fulfills the command of the passage, the one who forgives us for not doing what we should, or the one who is promised to us in the passage.

Ask for prayer requests, and encourage your kids to pray for each of those requests. You may want to use the church directory to pray for people in your church, or just pray for whoever you can think of. Be sure to pray with thankfulness to train your kids that there are things to be thankful for.

That's it. Easy as it can be. When you build this into the rhythm of your family, it will become a valuable time for your family to connect and gather around Jesus.

I get asked about the best time to do family worship. I think the important thing is to do it at a consistent time that works for all of you. If that's dinner, when you all are around the table, go for it. If it is at bedtime, that works as well. If you're a morning family, that's great as well.

One more thing: be consistent, but be flexible. Family worship will look different at times, and it will happen with different frequency, and that is okay. And when you forget or get lazy, don't beat yourself up over it—just get back to it. The point is not so much the time or frequency, but that you do it and do it regularly.

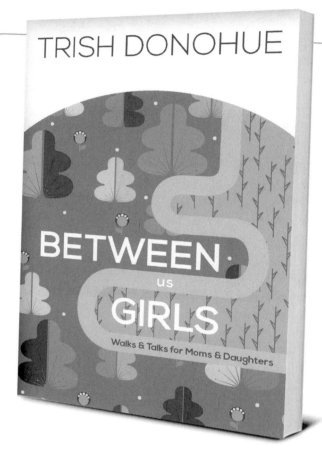

TRISH DONOHUE

BETWEEN us GIRLS

Walks & Talks for Moms & Daughters

Between Us Girls by Trish Donohoe is more than a devotional; it's a conversation guide, and the twenty-six "chats" are just the beginning. These gospel-driven talks are a fun and easy guide for mothers who want to disciple their daughters but don't know where to start.

NEW GROWTH PRESS

newgrowthpress.com